Routledge Revivals

A Social and Industrial History of England 1815-1918

First Published in 1920, *A Social and Industrial History of England 1815-1918* provides within as small a compass as possible, the historical background necessary for the study of modern industrial and social questions. An attempt has been made to show the interaction between political and economic development in the course of nineteenth century by correlating the growth of democratic institutions with the progress of industry. This book is an essential read for scholars and researchers of social history, industrial history, British history, and modern history in general.

A Social and Industrial History of England 1815-1918

J.F. Rees

Routledge
Taylor & Francis Group

First published in 1920
by Methuen & Co. Ltd

This edition first published in 2022 by Routledge
2 Park Square, Milton Park, Abingdon, Oxon, OX14 4RN
and by Routledge
605 Third Avenue, New York, NY 10017

Routledge is an imprint of the Taylor & Francis Group, an informa business

Publisher's Note
The publisher has gone to great lengths to ensure the quality of this reprint but points out that some imperfections in the original copies may be apparent.

Disclaimer
The publisher has made every effort to trace copyright holders and welcomes correspondence from those they have been unable to contact.

A Library of Congress record exists under LCCN:

ISBN: 978-1-032-18278-0 (hbk)
ISBN: 978-1-003-25376-1 (ebk)
ISBN: 978-1-032-18279-7 (pbk)

Book DOI 10.4324/9781003253761

A SOCIAL & INDUSTRIAL HISTORY OF ENGLAND 1815-1918

BY

J. F. REES, M.A.
FORMERLY SCHOLAR OF LINCOLN COLLEGE, OXFORD
LECTURER ON ECONOMIC HISTORY IN THE UNIVERSITY OF EDINBURGH

METHUEN & CO. LTD.
36 ESSEX STREET W.C.
LONDON

First Published in 1920

PREFACE

THE main purpose of this book is to provide, within as small a compass as possible, the historical background necessary for the study of modern industrial and social questions. An attempt has been made to show the interaction between political and economic development in the course of the nineteenth century by correlating the growth of democratic institutions with the progress of industry. The list of books in Appendix B. will serve as a guide to those who wish to follow up any particular question referred to in the text.

Since in dealing with recent history dates have a value for the general reader as a means of relating facts to others known to him, I have introduced them in the narrative and the index. I have also adopted the only consistent method of referring to persons—that is, to use their names without the conventional prefixes. Otherwise, I would have to take the responsibility of deciding every case on its merits.

J. F. R.

CONTENTS

APPENDICES

A SOCIAL AND INDUSTRIAL HISTORY OF ENGLAND
1815–1918

CHAPTER I

INTRODUCTORY

LIEUTENANT ICARUS B. WISE of the Royal Air Force was spending a few days' leave at his home, an old-fashioned farm-house in the heart of Berkshire. He had been telling the neighbours something about the exploits of airmen in France and Flanders. And after he had exhausted his experiences he found himself drawing upon his imagination for inventions which would have been resorted to had not the fighting come to a conclusion in November. These anticipations were received with much greater interest than his narrative of actual happenings. On the third evening of his stay he was sitting by himself before a cheerful fire, alternately thinking of his approaching return to civil life (in which he was a teacher of History) and dipping into an old favourite of his—Mr. H. G. Wells' *Time Machine*. In this romance, it will be remembered, a scientist designed a machine which could travel backwards and forwards through time, just as a ship, train, or aeroplane travels through space. As he was pondering rather drowsily, Lieutenant Wise suddenly recalled an experience which he had apparently forgotten, though it was in many ways more amazing than any he had related. He had been experimenting with an apparatus which would enable an observer, when he had reached a sufficiently high altitude, to switch his machine from climbing through space to rushing through time. His superior officers had not regarded his experiments with any great favour, though one had admitted that he could imagine that there would be some tactical advantage in being able to survey the battle-front as it would be in the middle of next week. Lieutenant Wise felt that this was meant to be sarcasm. He persisted, however, in his experiments, and was eventually ready for a trial trip. He could now very vividly recall how he had gone up alone, and, after he had climbed to the required altitude, had pulled over the time lever. For some reason or other he began going backwards through the centuries at an incredibly rapid rate. At first he was a little nervous and inclined to stop the time apparatus. But a glance at the country beneath him revealed such an extraordinary picture that he decided to go on. The whole of England and Wales was spread out under him like a map, and, in spite of the altitude, he could see the main details with remarkable clearness. He decided that he would observe every feature so minutely that his report on his return would convince the most sceptical of the success of his experiment. And so he travelled backwards until the indicator revealed that he was nearing the year 1350. At this point his eye caught the figure of a Franciscan friar walking across the fields from one village to another. It occurred to him at once that if he could effect a landing and persuade the friar to accompany him on the return journey, he would have definite corroboration of his report. In a moment he reverted to space and landed gracefully in a meadow. The friar, who was about a hundred yards away, stood his ground courageously, though inwardly he was commending himself to the Blessed Virgin and all the saints whose names he could recall. As he approached, Lieutenant Wise was greeted with a firm "*Pax vobiscum.*" Recalling some of the Latin he had learnt at school, he asked the friar to accompany him on his machine. To his surprise the invitation was accepted almost with resignation. He understood the friar to say that the countryside had been desolated by a terrible plague, and that he had been occupied with ministering to the sick and dying for months. Even now he was on his way to another village where most of the inhabitants were stricken; but if his hour was come, he was ready to enter the chariot of fire. On the return journey Lieutenant Wise gave the friar strict injunctions to notice everything that happened, so that his report could be compared in detail with his own. These reports he had quite forgotten to send in to his superiors. They were still in his pocket-book, and, taking them out, he read: "Report of Mathew of the Order of Friars Mendicant. IN NOMINE, etc. . . . AMEN. As I was wending my way from Godestow to Sagaeston I beheld a chariot driving through the sky. It came to earth nigh unto me, and the rider thereof bade me ascend with him. We mounted to the higher heavens, and (whether in the spirit or out of the spirit I know not) I beheld the kingdoms of the earth spread out beneath me. And he that was with me bade me look and mark all I saw, to the end that I should write it in a book. At first I saw little worthy to be recorded. Around the villages there were the great ploughed fields, the pasture, meadow, and wood thereof. The boroughs were confined within their walls, and the country was dotted with monasteries and castles. Then saw I some ploughed land turned into pasture and covered with flocks of sheep. To my sorrow I beheld the houses of the religious fall into decay. Many of the woods vanished, and great marshes seemed to be dried up as with a fervent heat. The boroughs crept out from their gates and straggled along the roads in disorderly array. For the greater part of my journey I witnessed nothing the significance of which passed my comprehension. Then towards the end came a sudden change. I beheld another world like unto Babylon the fallen, of which it is written that it is become the hold of every foul spirit. The boroughs now grew large and dense, disfiguring the earth, ever and anon hidden from my eyes by clouds of black smoke as from unquenchable fires. The great ploughed fields were cut up into small squares, all of which seemed to be hedged about with embankments. I saw dragons, from whose nostrils issued fire and smoke, speeding hither and thither, seeking what they might devour. All this must have been a vision of the terrors which await the wicked, for I cannot conceive that men could live in happiness amid such enormities."

Lieutenant Wise chuckled as he read Friar Mathew's narrative. It was so different from his own; and yet he felt that in some unaccountable way it was nearer to the truth of things. His own report seemed so stilted and commonplace by the side of it. "It was a perfect day for observation when I left the aerodrome, and my machine climbed to the necessary altitude without difficulty. I switched on the time apparatus, but in my excitement I used the reverse lever, and pulled it over so far that it jammed, and I began going back through time at a considerable speed. The first impression was extraordinarily like watching a cinema performance, with the recurrent words of explanation mercifully omitted. As I dashed back along the years, one handiwork of man after another disappeared. The great trunk railways broke up into local disconnected sections and then were obliterated. The network of canals remained a little longer, but they too were soon effaced. The main roads became irregular and narrow. The great industrial towns of the North contracted, became extremely dilapidated, and then passed into what were nothing more than straggling villages. The older towns withdrew inside their ancient boundaries. I noticed that there was no London south of the Thames. There seemed to be no considerable towns left. As far as I could judge, London, Bristol, and Norwich were the largest; but these, from our point of view, were quite small. In the country I saw enclosures and hedges obliterated, and in their place there were apparently large ploughed fields divided into long and narrow strips. I found myself by the time my indicator registered the year 1760 in a county of few industries, defective means of communication, and a comparatively small population. From that point until I landed in 1350 the journey was monotonous enough. I saw nothing of significance. The sleepiness of Old England appalled me."

It must be admitted that these two reports, when we remember the novelty of the experience and the strain under which the observation was conducted, do credit to the friar and the lieutenant. They agree that at some point the aspect of the country changed, and Lieutenant Wise, who could refer to his indicator, says it happened somewhere about 1760. Our two observers report that, prior to that change, the country bore much the same general appearance for centuries. Then occurred a revolution, during which a country came into existence which was entirely unintelligible to the friar. Into that country we have been born, and we are so familiar with its main features that we do not realize how modern it is. The history we usually learn deals with the older England. The two reports will enable us to summarize the changes which converted a country mainly agricultural into one predominantly industrial.

Notice, first, the references to the changes in the external appearance of the countryside. These must be interpreted by studying the history of the English village. We know that in the first part of the eighteenth century England remained, despite local enclosures of the sixteenth and seventeenth centuries, a country of "open fields." The arable was laid out in extensive unenclosed fields which were divided into acre strips (usually ten times as long as they were broad), separated from one another by a narrow balk of unploughed turf. The acres belonged to different tenants, but they were all cultivated according to common agreement. Tradition prescribed that any particular "open field" should be under wheat one year, barley the next, and then should lie fallow for a year before wheat was again sown in it. In addition there was common meadow, in which the tenants had a right to a share of the hay, and common pasture, open all the year round to those who enjoyed common rights, i.e. the right to graze a certain number of cattle, sheep, etc. All this was a survival of the manorial system which had prevailed in the Middle Ages. This method of cultivation was open to serious criticisms. It was so strongly ruled by tradition that an enterprising individual had no opportunity to make experiments. The strips in the "open fields" had to be cultivated by common agreement, and the presumption was always in favour of maintaining tradition. Until 1773 the unanimous consent of all the holders of strips was necessary before any change could be made. The opponents of the old system could point out that the strips were too narrow to allow of cross-ploughing or cross-harrowing; that the balks were covered with weeds, the seeds of which were scattered on the arable; and that it was a waste of time for an individual to cultivate strips scattered over all the "open fields" of the village. There were no hedges, for the arable and meadow were only temporarily enclosed for cereals and hay. When the harvest was in, all the cattle and sheep ranged freely everywhere. This made it difficult to cope with an outbreak of disease among them, or to improve the stock. The animals were undersized and insufficiently fed, for, until the introduction of turnips and artificial grasses, there was no adequate winter feed. The agricultural improvers were all strong advocates of enclosures; they held that no progress was possible until each proprietor surrendered his bundle of rights in the "open fields," meadow, and pasture, and received in return a compact holding. They proposed, in short, to substitute for the old English village a number of separate farms, which the proprietors were required to enclose with the hedges which now give a distinctive character to our scenery. This change was effected by means of private Acts of Parliament, usually promoted by the wealthiest proprietors and passed without difficulty through a Parliament which was then virtually controlled by the landed interest. Under the power of an Act enclosure commissioners would literally redraw the map of the village, obliterating nearly all the features which had come down from antiquity. The social consequences of these changes were far-reaching. The old village with all its faults was a community. Its organic nature had not been entirely lost. A great number of people had contrived to live on small holdings with the assistance of the rights of common. For these enclosures offered no compensations. Those who did not become landless labourers left the countryside to increase the congestion in the growing industrial centres. Ultimately, then, the acute division of opinion on the question of enclosures turns on the treatment of rights of common. Was their extinction inevitable? If so, were the classes which depended on them fully considered and justly treated? Enclosure may have been a necessary step in the improvement of agriculture, but the process placed an intolerable strain on those least able to bear it. Arthur Young, himself a most ardent preacher of the gospel of improvement, gives us a glimpse in 1801 of an enclosed village. "Go to an ale-house kitchen of an old enclosed country, and there you will see the origin of poverty and poor rates. For whom are they to be sober? For whom are they to save? (Such are their questions.) For the parish? If I am diligent, shall I have leave to build a cottage? If I am sober, shall I have land for a cow? If I am frugal, shall I have half an acre for potatoes? You offer no motives; you have nothing but a parish officer and a workhouse! Bring me another pot."[1]

[1] Young, *An Inquiry into the Propriety of Applying Wastes, etc.*, 1801; quoted in *English Economic History: Select Documents*, p. 536.

If we turn back to the two reports on which we are commenting, it will be noticed that Lieutenant Wise describes the country before 1760 as one of few industries. The friar, on the other hand, is so thunderstruck by what he witnessed in Modern England that he cannot find words with which to describe it. In 1760 there was, as a matter of fact, one considerable industry in the country, but it assumed forms which are no longer familiar to us. This was the woollen industry, which had long been fostered by English policy as the staple industry. To find new markets for woollen goods, attempts had been made to discover northern routes to the East, because there was little demand for them in the tropical and sub-tropical countries touched on the Cape route to India. To safeguard the interests of this industry steps were taken to prevent the export of woollens from Ireland and the American colonies. The Lord Chancellor of England, it will be remembered, sits on the Woolsack. The industry still remained in the domestic stage which it had assumed towards the end of the Middle Ages. Spinning was done, particularly by women and children, throughout the country in their own homes. The distribution of wool and the collection of yarn was organized by merchant middlemen, who were the typical capitalists of the period. Weaving was more definitely localized in three main districts: (1) The West of England, especially Wiltshire and Somersetshire; (2) the Eastern Counties, with important centres at Norwich and Colchester; and (3) the West Riding of Yorkshire. But this specialization is hardly comparable with that of modern times. There were no large industrial cities. Norwich, the largest woollen city, with a population of between 30,000 and 40,000, was little more than a market for " the throng of villages," by which

Daniel Defoe says it was surrounded. The weavers worked in their own houses, owning or paying for the use of their hand-looms. They were rarely entirely dependent on their earnings at the loom, for they usually cultivated a small holding as well. In fact, weaving was almost necessarily a by-employment when spinning was done by hand, because the supply of yarn was insufficient.

No other industry can compare with the woollen in importance and extent. Iron-smelting was decaying within the country, for it was dependent on charcoal, which is produced from timber. Alarm had long been felt at the destruction of trees for this purpose, and it had been restricted in the interests of shipbuilding. The old centres of iron-smelting were the Weald, the Forest of Dean, and Shropshire, the localization depending on the supply of wood. Parliament, however, had encouraged the production of pig and bar iron in Ireland and the American colonies.

A word must be said about the defective means of communication in the middle of the eighteenth century. The country was then vastly larger, in the sense that it took much longer to go from one place to another. Contemporaries mostly agree with Arthur Young that the roads were "execrable," many of them being quite unsuited for wheeled traffic. In 1754 a "flying coach" was advertised to travel from Manchester to London in four days and a half. The conveyance of heavy goods was practically impossible. And there were other perils besides broken axles. The Portsmouth mail was stolen in 1757 at Hammersmith before it entered London. Hounslow Heath was notorious for its footpads. No doubt the roads were greatly improved under the provisions of local Turnpike Acts, but there was no elaborate road-building until the days of Telford and Macadam, that is, until the first two decades of the nineteenth century.

To the changes which came over England in the latter part of the eighteenth century Arnold Toynbee has taught us to apply the name of the Industrial Revolution. In his lectures he set the limits of the Revolution at 1760 and 1840, but later writers have tended to restrict it to a shorter period. M. Paul Mantoux, for instance, confines his treatment to the years 1760 to 1800, on the ground that the technical inventions and improvements which marked the Revolution fall within these years. There seems to be some incongruity in speaking of a "revolution" which lasted eighty or even forty years. The word is usually applied to a political change of a catastrophic nature, and does not in popular usage include the far-reaching consequences of the event. No one speaks of the English Revolution of 1688 as extending to 1832, though in a very real sense the settlement made by the Whigs under William III survived until the passing of the Reform Bill. Similarly, we think of the French Revolution as a movement of limited duration, in spite of the fact that its consequences are apparent in all civilized communities at the present day. In a broad sense no limit can yet be set to the Industrial Revolution; we are still going through the series of readjustments that were started by the industrial changes of the latter part of the eighteenth century. But a distinction may be drawn between the Revolution and its consequences. If we agree that a revolution implies a sudden and fairly complete disintegration of what existed before it, we may choose the years 1760 to 1800, for then the old order received the full force of the shock. A revolution, however, also involves some attempted reintegration, for human society must adopt some more or less stable form if it is to survive at all. This reconstruction (as we would now call it) was delayed, because the wars against the French Republic and Napoleon distracted attention from domestic problems and led the Government to use repressive measures whenever any difficulties arose.

It is convenient in discussing the Industrial Revolution to treat it (1) as an improvement in the technique of production, (2) as an extension of markets, necessarily involving better means of communication, and (3) in its social reactions. In improved technique the textile industries led the way. The first important invention was James Hargreaves' spinning-jenny (1764), which was a device by which eight spindles were combined, thereby multiplying a simple process. In 1769 Richard Arkwright patented his water-frame, by which non-human motive power (at first, water) could be applied to spinning. With Samuel Crompton's mule (1779), which combined the principles of the spinning-jenny and the water-frame, the machine was evolved which is still the basis of that used in the textile factories of the world. These inventions virtually introduced the cotton industry into the country, for prior to 1760 it was of slight importance. Cotton was, in fact, *the* industry of the Revolution. There are several reasons for this: the industry was not fettered by all the regulations which had been elaborated to foster the woollen industry; the supply of raw cotton from the United States was enormously increased after Eli Whitney perfected his cotton-gin (1793) which cleaned the fibre from seeds; and naturally in the East there was a much more extensive market for cheap cottons than for woollens of any kind. In the iron industry the important inventions were chemical rather than mechanical.

Abraham Darby, a member of a Shropshire family of iron masters, solved the fuel problem at Coalbrookdale by treating coal as the charcoal-burners treated wood; the resultant coke was suitable for smelting iron. It was now possible to turn out increasing quantities of pig-iron. The conversion of cast into wrought iron still presented difficulties, which were not removed until the process of puddling was discovered (1783–4), independently and within a year of one another, by Henry Cort, an Admiralty contractor at Gosport, and Peter Onions, a foreman in the Merthyr Tydvil Ironworks. These discoveries were followed by mechanical inventions. Cort himself invented a rolling mill. Dr. John Roebuck of the famous Carron Ironworks experimented with the blast furnace, producing a continuous blast by means of engines driven by water-power in 1761. James Watt (1736–1819) installed one of his steam-engines in these works when the water supply was becoming inadequate; the engine, however, was not directly attached to the mechanism which produced the blast, but employed to pump back the water already used into the reservoir for further use. The improvement of the steam-engine finally connected up all machine industries and effected the interdependence of coal, iron, and textiles. In its origins the steam-engine was—as is shown in the example already quoted—essentially a pump. The direct application of steam-power to the driving of machinery was the great contribution of James Watt to industrial development. As the result of a series of experiments on the pressure of steam, he invented an engine which had a separate condenser and was consequently a great improvement on all previous models. Associated with Dr. John Roebuck, as long as he controlled the Carron Works, he found a second and more influential patron in Matthew Boulton of the Soho Works, Birmingham. There he pursued his experiments, patenting in 1782 the double-acting engine, which produced a continuous rotative action. This engine could be directly applied to the running of machinery.

The expansion of the market is necessarily demanded by an increase in the production of commodities. This is largely a question of improving the existing means of communication and of discovering new ones. During the first part of the eighteenth century commerce had made considerable progress; this, indeed, may be regarded as the chief stimulus to the adoption of the new inventions. England had attained the premier place in foreign trade before she became the home of the great industries; she was a "nation of shopkeepers" before she became the "workshop of the world." Improvement in internal communications to facilitate the conveyance of large quantities of heavy commodities, such as coal, was effected by the building of canals. The first canal in England was constructed from Worsley to Manchester with the express object of carrying the Duke of Bridgewater's coal. It was planned and executed by James Brindley, an untrained engineer whose flashes of genius enabled him to surmount all difficulties. The success of the Bridgewater Canal—the price of coal in Manchester fell to one-half of what it had been—marked the beginning of a period during which speculators, infected with "canal mania," projected many canals which had no prospect of justifying the expenditure on them. "The internal markets," writes M. Mantoux,[1] "formerly so

[1] Paul Mantoux, *La Revolution Industrielle*, pp. 117–8. This detailed study of the Revolution has not yet been translated. I have ventured to quote this passage in English.

restricted, were now connected with one another. At the end of the eighteenth century there could be seen on the great canals, as, for instance, that of the Trent and Mersey, a variety of commodities from all districts: salt from Cheshire, coal from Wigan and Newcastle, cast-iron from the Upper Severn, and iron and copper goods from Wolverhampton and Birmingham. In the first rank figured coal; everywhere branches connected to the trunk canals reached the mines, the producer was encouraged to exploit new coal measures, and the consumer, because of its low price, to adapt it to new uses."

The working out of the changes here briefly summarized, and the inevitable effect on the life of the people constitute the *Social and Industrial History* of the nineteenth century. The population of England and Wales, which had been increasing at a slow rate for centuries, doubled itself between 1750 and 1830. It was also redistributed. In the older England the bulk of the population lived in the south-eastern plain because the country was mainly agricultural. The north-west was then pastoral and sparsely populated. The Industrial Revolution turned the balance, for coal and iron were mostly found in the north-west. This displacement of population is an important social fact.[1] It meant the uprooting of men and women from surroundings, with which they were familiar and where they were protected by the traditional sanctions of religion and neighbourliness, and the transplanting of them among strangers as bewildered as themselves by their experiences. The

[1] Cobden and Bright may be taken as typical Lancashire men; yet Cobden was born at Heyshott in Sussex, where his family had long been settled on the land; the Brights sprang originally from Lyneham in North Wiltshire. These are only two well-authenticated examples of the extensive displacement.

new aggregates lacked tradition and self-respect. The industrial system also created the wage-earner, or, at any rate, made the wage-earner the chief type. Before 1760 the pure wage-earner was exceptional. There were comparatively few who were completely separated from the land and dependent for their living on finding employment in a factory where the only connexion with their employer was what Carlyle called the " cash nexus."

CHAPTER II

WAR AND PEACE

IN 1815 Great Britain emerged from a war which had lasted, with slight intermissions, for nearly quarter of a century. During these years the country had also been experiencing the consequences of the changes which are comprehended under the term Industrial Revolution. So to understand the problems of the years of peace immediately following Waterloo it is necessary to form some conception of industrial developments as they were affected by the abnormal conditions arising out of the war. It is generally recognized that the country was able to endure the strain of the long struggle because it had discovered new means of multiplying the production of commodities. The tendency is therefore to regard the Industrial Revolution as an unexpected ally which fortunately came to the assistance of Great Britain and defeated every effort of her enemies to reduce her to submission. The analogy is fairly apt. It must be remembered, however, that allies do not generally come out of a war unscathed. They have to adjust themselves to co-operate with others, to make calls on their own resources, and to endure the strain of reversion to peace conditions when the war is over. To attempt to interpret the industrial changes without constant reference to the abnormal features of the period would therefore lead to misrepresentation. The problems of 1815 to 1819 are to be traced to the peculiar twist given to the Industrial Revolution by the exigencies of the war. It would be unprofitable to conjecture what course events might have taken had not Great Britain been involved in war from 1793 to 1815; but it is surely significant that practically all the decisions which had in them the root of future trouble had to be taken under the stress of immediate necessity to meet difficulties which were due to the war.

The year 1795, for instance, was one of great distress, the price of wheat rising to 108s. a quarter. There were food riots in many parts of the country, the mobs seizing the supplies of the shopkeepers and selling them at what they considered to be a fair price. The Government, however, did not meet this crisis either by controlling the supply and fixing the prices of necessaries, or by adopting means to adjust wages to the rise in the cost of living. The latter solution was suggested by Samuel Whitbread, a Radical member of the House of Commons, who introduced a minimum wage Bill, which was in form an explanation and amendment of an Elizabethan Act, by which justices of the peace were empowered to assess the local rate of wages. On its second reading the Bill was strongly opposed by Pitt, who, as a student of Adam Smith's *Wealth of Nations*, insisted that it was better to rely on the unrestricted operation of general principles. They should look, he is reported as saying, to the instances where interference had shackled industry, and where the best intentions have often produced the most pernicious effects. It was indeed the most absurd bigotry, in asserting the general principle, to exclude the exception; but trade, industry, and barter would always find their own level, and be impeded by regulations which violated their natural operation and deranged their proper effect. The result of this speech was that the second reading was negatived without a division. The prestige of the Prime Minister was so great that many who imperfectly followed his exposition of the *laissez-faire* principles of the new political economy supported him in resisting the adoption of a minimum wage. Unfortunately, however, the unrestricted operation of principles did not eliminate the problem; the question of adjusting wages to high prices remained. The refusal of Parliament to deal with it merely meant that it was left to the local authorities. On 6 May, 1795, the Berkshire justices of the peace had met at the Pelican Inn in Speenhamland, and, having recommended employers to raise wages, went on completely to nullify the effect of their recommendation by agreeing that low wages should be supplemented out of the parish funds. They drew up a scale of the wages a single man, a married man, or a married man with one or more children should receive as the selling price of the gallon loaf rose and fell. If he was not in receipt of the proper amount as wages, it was to be made up out of the parish funds for him. But first he had to become a pauper. The inevitable result was that the majority of agricultural labourers became paupers, and were quite indifferent as to what proportion of their weekly wage was paid by their employers and what was an allowance from the parish. The labourer who wished to remain independent was therefore at a disadvantage in competing with subsidized able-bodied paupers. The Speenhamland example was so generally followed that by 1834 it was known in every county in England and Wales, except Northumberland and Durham.

The Allowance System—as this practice came to

be called—is a characteristic expression of the paternal traditions of government which still influenced the landed class. Paternal government, which consists in doing something for the people but not allowing them to do anything for themselves, necessarily alternates between somewhat misguided benevolence and repressive measures. The justices of the peace were not so open to conviction on the question of non-intervention as the House of Commons, and they could argue from their personal knowledge that something had to be done. So they really adopted the principle of a minimum wage, but provided it, not by forcing the employers to pay it directly, but by drawing on the poor rates to supplement existing wages. The problem of able-bodied pauperism, which presented serious difficulties in the after-war period, was therefore the direct result of the mismanagement of a situation primarily due to war conditions.

While the landed interest retained some of the traditions of paternal rule the new order of manufacturers was disposed to accept the principles of non-intervention. The Industrial Revolution made in the direction of a larger productive unit equipped with machinery which became more and more expensive. Consequently, there emerged a class of manufacturers controlling and directing industry. To it belonged those who, for a variety of reasons, achieved success in the new ventures. Generally speaking, they had business capacity but little or no knowledge of technical processes. It might be expected that the chief inventors would be found among them; but no successful business was established by Hargreaves, Crompton, Cartwright, or Cort, and James Watt owed his success to Matthew Boulton. The apparent exception is that of Richard Arkwright; but curiously enough, doubt has been thrown on his claim to be the true inventor of his patents. All that can be said of the chief industrial magnates is that they sprang from the class of small farmers which was disappearing in the eighteenth century. As far as they had a conscious political policy it was to support the removal of all restrictions on industry ; their self-interest tending to give a strong practical backing to the doctrine of *laissez-faire*. At the same time the wage-earners were stumbling towards a self-consciousness. They displayed a natural hostility towards the new inventions and in many cases violently destroyed them. The machine, it seemed to them, would deprive the artisan's skill of its economic value. This was the first obvious effect of its introduction. In the long run larger production would mean cheaper goods, wider markets, more extensive industries, and a greater demand for labour ; but the displaced workman could hardly be expected to take this view of the process which deprived him of his immediate means of livelihood. Worse still was the case of the domestic workers who tried to maintain the losing fight against the competition of machine production. The artisans saw one after another of their guarantees against exploitation disappear. The practice of assessing wages locally according to the provisions of the Elizabethan Act was abandoned about the middle of the eighteenth century, and, in any case, was held not to apply to the new industries. The apprenticeship regulations, also resting on parliamentary enactment, were allowed to fall into desuetude. So the wage-earners had to begin a long struggle to establish a new system of safeguards. In the first phase their difficulties were practically insuperable. It is true that they had the example of organization in the old-established crafts, but any attempt to form a combination, such as a trade club, was strongly opposed by the employers and in danger of being denounced as illegal. Here again the position was further complicated by the war. On the one hand, there were violent fluctuations in prices which naturally created a demand for increased wages; on the other hand, the Government was obsessed with the idea that French revolutionary opinions might spread among the wage-earners, and therefore could not contemplate without alarm any common action on their part. The Combination Laws of 1799 and 1800 were passed partly under the influence of these fears. Workmen were forbidden to organize either in order to raise wages or to shorten the hours of labour. Putting together the Combination Laws and the common law regarding conspiracy, Professor Dicey makes the following broad generalization of their effect: "Any artisan who organized a strike or joined a trade union was a criminal and liable on conviction to imprisonment; the strike was a crime, the trade union was an unlawful association."[1] In spite of the law and the severity with which it was administered, combinations were in fact frequently formed; but they were always in danger of being denounced to the authorities by employers or betrayed by informers. The natural desire of workmen to combine with their fellows was therefore suppressed, with the twofold consequence that the secret organizations often dabbled in revolutionary plots and the working-class movement was deprived of the stability which it might have gained from legitimate trade unionism. So the position became critical in the years of trade depression following the peace of 1815. Many employers argued that

[1] Dicey, *Law and Opinion in England*, p. 98.

prices were so low that a reduction of wages would not involve any hardship. Their attitude provoked strikes and combinations with the attendant prosecutions throughout the country. The operation of the Combination Laws was an important factor in the acute unrest of those years.

In the speech already referred to Pitt drew attention to what could be done by the employment of children, and asked the House "to consider the weight which their support by their own labours took off the country, and the addition which, by the fruits of their toil, and the habits to which they were formed, was made to its internal opulence." He has often been taken to task for this complacent allusion to what was the most serious blot on British industry. But here again it is only fair to ascribe the brutality towards children in some measure to war conditions. Self-seeking persons saw their opportunity of making money by setting up cotton mills and installing machinery which could be tended by children. As long as water-power was used the localization of these mills was governed by the consideration of securing a good and constant supply. So they were often erected in remote places far from the centres of population. The question of obtaining labour therefore presented difficulties. When David Dale built his cotton factories at New Lanark to take advantage of the River Clyde he failed to induce any of the surrounding rural population to enter them. He was glad to accept the labour of some shipwrecked sailors, but finally adopted the system of introducing orphan and pauper children. This expedient, which was a kind of perversion of the old apprenticeship methods, appealed to many who were less scrupulous than David Dale. The unfortunate children, obtained in batches—often with a premium—from the parish authorities, were herded together under appalling conditions; they lived and slept in the mills, and were seriously overworked. Outbreaks of epidemics among them drew attention to the abuses of the system. Dr. Percival (1740–1804) of Manchester took up the cause of the pauper children and began an agitation against handing them over to mill-owners. The result was the "Health and Morals of Apprentices Act" of 1802, which is often called the first Factory Act. It limited the working day of apprentices to twelve hours, provided that night-work should cease in June, 1804, and required that the children should be taught reading, writing, and arithmetic. Other clauses prescribed the regular whitewashing of factories, proper ventilation, and adequate sleeping accommodation. But the weakness of the Act was that its enforcement was entrusted to the local justices of the peace, who were empowered to inflict fines not exceeding £5 for any breach of its provisions. The Act was in fact virtually a dead-letter. The employment of pauper children was abandoned not so much because of the outcry against its abuse as because, with the adoption of steam-power, factories were concentrated in urban areas where an ample supply of child labour could be secured without assuming the reponsibilities of housing, feeding, and clothing them. The Act of 1802 was so restricted—it only applied to pauper apprentices in cotton mills and was as much a poor-law regulation as a Factory Act—and so ineffective that it was of little immediate significance; but regarded in the light of later developments it shows that Parliament could be induced to intervene on humanitarian grounds when a definite abuse was exposed. The important fact to remember is that the abuse of child labour survived the war;

and the temper and outlook of the next generation must be judged in the light of its upbringing.

War withdraws from productive labour a considerable proportion of the adult men on whose shoulders the chief burden of maintaining the industrial fabric normally rests. In the later stages of the war there were about half a million men serving in the army; the strength of the navy was increased from 50,000 in 1803 to 112,000 in 1814. At the same time the demand for commodities increased, partly because the Government by means of taxation and loans assumed a special spending power which ultimately reached more than £100,000,000 a year, and partly because the control of the seas gave Great Britain access to markets from which other belligerents were excluded. In the course of the war the volume of British foreign trade was doubled, cotton goods and iron manufactured articles showing the greatest increase. The adoption of machinery and the employment of women and children as well as the men who were not serving with the forces made this great output possible. It must not be supposed that this prosperity, artificial as it was, suffered no checks during the war period; much of the foreign trade was highly speculative and liable to acute depression at times. The end of the war, however, was followed by serious dislocation. Robert Owen put one aspect of it very well when he remarked that on the day on which peace was signed the great customer of the producers died. The State with its vast war expenditure went off the market. The effect was at once felt by those who were producing food, clothing, and munitions to meet its demands. The price of copper fell from £180 to £80 and iron from £20 to £8 a ton. The distress in the South Wales iron districts was so great that rioting broke out in several places, particularly in Merthyr Tydvil, where the military had to be called out. The men alleged that their wages had been reduced to six shillings a week, which, since food prices were high, was below subsistence level; so they formed themselves into companies and marched from place to place, putting out blast furnaces and inducing others to stop work. In the metal-working districts of the Midlands the employers were forced to adopt short-time and in many instances to close down altogether. This naturally reacted on coal mining. The South Staffordshire colliers attempted to draw attention to their destitution by harnessing themselves to wagons filled with coal which they dragged to London, Liverpool, and other towns, declaring that they were willing to work but refused to beg. The depression soon extended to the textile industries. Great stocks of manufactured goods had been accumulated with a view to flooding the foreign markets as soon as the war was over. These had to be sold at ruinous prices, because the countries which had been involved in the war were too poor to buy and also anxious to establish industries of their own. George Philips, a well-known Manchester manufacturer, was of opinion that during the war events had led to the establishment of industries, "the very existence of which just reasoning shows must be disadvantageous to the country. But the manufactures, having once been established, capitals engaged in them, and many inhabitants of the country become dependent on them for subsistence, they cannot be abandoned without great mischief. Having acted on a bad principle, we cannot recede from it, and must still go on even after we are convinced of our mistake." [1]

[1] Quoted by Smart, *Economic Annals*, vol. i. 491 n., from *Hansard*, xxix. 810.

Great Britain had, according to this view, taken advantage of the special circumstances of the war period to develop her industrial resources as against the rest of the world to an excessive degree. The widespread unemployment which was due to industrial depression was greatly exaggerated by the demobilization of the army and navy. It is estimated that about 500,000 were liberated from the services between 1814 and 1816. These went to swell the numbers in the industrial market when it was already overstocked.

The state of agriculture, however, at first excited more alarm than the industrial situation. Here again war conditions had created a serious problem. Before the Industrial Revolution England was in normal years not only self-sufficing but actually exported surplus supplies of corn. This ceased to be the case in the latter part of the eighteenth century, when the growth of population balanced home demand and supply in good years. This meant a shortage in bad seasons and a rise in prices, which could only be moderated by importation. The war cut off foreign supplies, and the home demand became so great that the area under cultivation rapidly extended. Corn was raised from land which would only repay cultivation in abnormal circumstances. Generally speaking, high prices ruled throughout the period and agriculture enjoyed unwonted prosperity; good profits were made by tenant-farmers, landlords raised rents, and banks advanced money for investment in improvements. The prosperity was regarded as stable, and farmers adjusted their expenditure to the new conditions. The Speenhamland system checked the demand for higher wages, though it obviously greatly increased the burden of the poor rates. In 1814 there was some alarm as to the possible effect of the end of the war ; it was feared that the importation of corn from the Baltic and the United States would bring down the prices. Accordingly the famous Corn Law of 1815 was passed by which it was provided that no foreign corn should enter the country until the price of home-grown wheat rose above 80s. a quarter. The harvest of 1815 turned out to be good, and the result was disastrous, for the home supply was so abundant that prices fell. The farmers were paying enhanced rents and had much of their capital invested in the land, and consequently were unable to meet their obligations to their landlords and the banks. Within a year, however, the situation completely changed. The harvest of 1816 was almost a complete failure. The price of corn went up, but the farmers had comparatively little to sell. Consequently high prices proved as ruinous as low. The following three seasons were bad. Much corn land which had been cultivated during the war reverted to pasture, farm labourers were thrown out of work, and the general scarcity provoked disorders all over the country.

The Whigs ascribed the distress to the excessive burden of taxation. In the course of the war the revenue raised by taxation had been increased from seventeen to over sixty-eight millions. The bulk of this was levied by means of indirect taxes, there being a prejudice against a direct tax based on assessment of income. It was not until the seventh year of the war that Pitt decided to impose an income-tax which he represented to be of a purely temporary nature. The tax continued in force until the end of the war, when the outcry against it was so strong that the Government failed to carry its proposal that it should be continued at half the war rate. Its total repeal meant that the burden of indirect taxes could not be lightened. The

Chancellor of the Exchequer had to retain the multitude of taxes, which are best described in the often quoted passage from Sydney Smith's article in the *Edinburgh Review* : " taxes upon every article which enters into the mouth, or covers the back, or is placed under the foot—taxes upon everything which it is pleasant to see, hear, feel, smell or taste—taxes upon warmth, light, locomotion—taxes on everything on earth, and the waters under the sea—on everything that comes from abroad or is grown at home—taxes on raw material—taxes on every fresh value that is added to it by the industry of man—taxes on the sauce which pampers a man's appetite, and the drug that restores him to health—on the ermine which decorates the judge, and the rope which hangs the criminal—on the poor man's salt, and the rich man's spice—on the brass nails of the coffin, and the ribands of the bride—at bed or board, couchant or levant, we must pay."

The denunciation of taxes was well calculated to meet with general approbation. The evils of depreciated paper money, however, were not recognized. It was, indeed, persistently denied that there was any depreciation, and the Government had persuaded the House of Commons in 1811 to adopt a resolution to that effect in the face of weighty evidence to the contrary. At a moment of crisis in 1797 the Bank of England had been ordered to suspend cash payments—that is, it was forbidden to make any payments in cash. The payment of debts in bank-notes was to be deemed as payment in cash, if offered and accepted as such. The adoption of inconvertible paper money, rather than her increasing productive capacity, seemed to many contemporaries to be the real secret of Great Britain's staying-power during the long war. The right to issue notes, which the Bank was not required to convert into gold on demand, was cautiously employed until about 1809, when the apparent appreciation of bullion and the fall in the rate of exchange suggested that there might be an over-issue. Ricardo (1772–1823) stated this view in a series of letters to the *Morning Chronicle* which he afterwards collected under the title of "The High Price of Bullion, a Proof of the Depreciation of Bank Notes." The Report of the Bullion Committee of 1810 supported the opinion that there was an excessive issue of paper money. Many bankers and merchants, however, held that there could not be an over-issue so long as the Bank made advances to meet the requirements of sound commercial transactions. They overlooked the effect of unduly adding to the volume of the currency. It has already been noticed that the Government refused to act as the Bullion Committee recommended. The rejection of the Report was followed by an Act which forbade all differences between payment in paper and in coin, and it was not until 1819 that it was resolved to resume cash payments. What part the over-issue of inconvertible paper money played in the fluctuations of prices it is difficult to ascertain; the Bullion Committee itself did not explore this problem. William Cobbett, who wrote articles in his *Political Register* in 1810 and 1811 on "Paper against Gold," and throughout his life tried to inculcate an opposition to paper money among the masses, set the debased state of the currency side by side with the weight of taxation as causes of the distress of the post-war period.[1]

[1] Cobbett was against paper money, whether convertible or inconvertible. The whole controversy as carried on by the supporters of the Bullion Report was so highly technical that Cobbett's views certainly did more to influence popular opinion than their arguments. The Reformers had in Thomas Atwood

The Liverpool Ministry confessed its failure to cope with the problems of the reversion to peace conditions by adopting measures of the greatest severity in a vain attempt to suppress all agitation without making any proper inquiry into its causes. It took advantage of the Spa Fields riot—a foolish demonstration by a group of extremists in December, 1816—to appoint secret Parliamentary Committees to examine the activities of reform societies and clubs. The Committees made alarmist reports, alleging that there was a traitorous conspiracy to overthrow the established government and effect a redistribution of property by means of a general insurrection. In the face of this supposed danger the Ministry suspended the Habeas Corpus Act and introduced an Act "to empower His Majesty to secure and detain such persons as His Majesty shall suspect are conspiring against his person and Government." It was to petition against the suspension of the Habeas Corpus Act that the march of the "Blanketeers" from Manchester to London was projected; but the demonstrators, provided with knapsacks and blankets, failed completely to carry out their design. The Government affected to believe that the scheme was a further proof of the ramifications of the revolutionary movement. They were actually confounding quite legitimate reform propaganda with the opinions of a mere handful who were followers of Thomas Spence, an advocate of the nationalization of land. And their attitude naturally provoked violence of language at least from speakers such as Henry Hunt,[1] usually

of Birmingham a convinced advocate of paper money as a panacea for all social ills. In 1832 Cobbett had a public debate with him on the question at Birmingham.

[1] Henry Hunt (1773–1835) was a member of a Wiltshire family. His father intended him for the Church, but he preferred farming. He was constantly involved in quarrels and

called "Orator" Hunt, who addressed working-class audiences in favour of parliamentary reform. He was to be the chief speaker at the ill-starred meeting which assembled in St. Peter's Fields, Manchester, on the morning of 16 August, 1819. Nearly 80,000 people marched in procession to take part in this great Radical demonstration, bearing banners on which "No Corn Laws," "Vote by Ballot," and "Equal Representation or Death" figured prominently. Hunt had already begun to speak when the magistrates resolved to effect his arrest. The police, assisted by a small body of the Cheshire Yeomanry, took Hunt and some other leaders without difficulty. Apparently the Yeomanry seemed to have some difficulty in returning, and the command was given to the Hussars and the remaining Yeomanry held in reserve to charge the crowd with their sabres. A terrible panic ensued, in which 8 persons were killed and 400 injured, including 113 women. The stupid blunder of the responsible magistrates was not only condoned by the Government, but actually commended. The Secretary of State communicated to them the thanks of the Prince Regent for their "prompt, decisive, and efficient measures." Hunt was condemned to two and a half years' imprisonment. The Government continued their repressive policy, putting on the Statute Book the infamous "Six Acts," which, it has been said, amounted to a sus-

lawsuits. In 1797 he left one troop of Yeomanry because it would not consent to serve outside the country, and joined another, from which he was discharged for challenging his superior officer to fight a duel. He was committed to prison in 1810 for assaulting a gamekeeper. There he enjoyed a good deal of licence and shared a room with William Cobbett, who was also serving a sentence. Hunt subsequently contested Bristol, Westminster, and other constituencies as an advanced Radical. He was returned for Preston in 1830, his programme including voting by ballot, universal suffrage, and annual parliaments.

pension of the Constitution. This code practically forbade all public meetings of a political character, strengthened the law against seditious libels, imposed a heavy stamp duty on all pamphlets sold for less than sixpence, prohibited unauthorized drilling, and gave the magistrates more extensive powers in searching for and seizing arms. The tragedy of Peterloo, however, had broken the spell. "And this was what these poor Manchester operatives, with all the darkness that was in them and around them, did manage to perform. They put their huge inarticulate question, What do you mean to do with us? in a manner audible to every reflective soul in this kingdom; exciting deep pity in all good men, deep anxiety in all men whatever; and no conflagration or outburst of madness came to cloud that feeling anywhere, but everywhere it operates unclouded. All England heard the question: it is the first practical form of our Sphinx-riddle. England will answer it; or on the whole England will perish;—one does not yet expect the latter result!"[1]

[1] Thomas Carlyle, *Past and Present* (1843), chap. iii.

CHAPTER III

REFORM

ONE important effect of the war was that it gave a new lease of life to the unreformed House of Commons. In fact, the whole question of reform was indefinitely postponed, and those who tried to reopen it were in danger of being denounced as enemies of their country. Prior to the war William Pitt had recognized that the anomalies of parliamentary representation were indefensible; but after 1793 he came to the conclusion that national stability demanded the maintenance of the system which in practice gave the chief political power to a group of great landed families. It had been estimated that 154 individuals enjoyed the right of returning 307 members to the House of Commons—that is, a majority of the House. To illustrate the anomalies it need only be remembered that Cornwall returned 44 members while Scotland had 45. The increase and displacement of population, which accompanied the Industrial Revolution, accentuated the inequalities of the distribution of seats: Lancashire, the country most profoundly affected, had only fourteen members. Old Sarum, with some seven burgage holders, returned its two members, as did also the fourteen voters of the borough of Dunwich, the site of which had almost been swept away by coast erosion. Leeds, Birmingham, and Manchester were not represented in Parliament. And it was not merely a question of bad distribution: the franchise was often restricted to a small minority whose votes were openly bought and sold. This system ensured the control of the ruling class over a sufficient number of constituencies to achieve their purposes.

The protest against these abuses had been gaining in strength prior to the outbreak of the French Revolution. Excesses in France were then held to constitute a case against reform, and after Great Britain declared war in 1793 it became comparatively easy to represent all political agitation at home as revolutionary or unpatriotic. To Pitt's mind the external danger was so great that internal unity had to be maintained by adopting the strongest measures against reformers. On the whole, popular opinion supported this repressive policy. The Government, indeed, might well have relied on this prevailing feeling and thereby saved itself from much worry and later opprobrium. It would have lost nothing by treating the advocates of reform with greater leniency. A war which lasted for nearly a quarter of a century naturally passed through many phases. As it neared its close it took on the character of a struggle against Napoleon's military dictatorship of Europe. The principle of liberty was invoked against tyranny, and reform again raised its head. The old stalwarts saw that the time had come to revive the agitation. In 1812 the Hampden Club was founded, and the veteran reformer, Major John Cartwright (brother of the inventor of the power-loom), formed the Union for Parliamentary Reform. These movements in London were imitated in the provinces, and local political organizations were more or less prepared for the outburst of agitation which followed the return to peace.

The movement which sprang out of the experiences of the years 1815–9 owed comparatively little to the older school of reformers. Major Cartwright, Sir Francis Burdett, and their supporters could hardly adjust themselves to the new conditions. Their somewhat pedantic presentation of the case for reform did not appeal to the industrial classes. The new emphasis was not so much on the anomalies of existing representation as on the social reconstruction which might be achieved through the reform of the House of Commons. The idea that political reform was a means towards social reform dominated working-class opinion from 1815 until the virtual collapse of Chartism in 1848. William Cobbett (1766–1835) did more than any other man to instil this belief. He was peculiarly fitted for the task, and the fact that he had strongly denied that peace would bring prosperity naturally told in his favour. Cobbett had had a varied experience. Born in the parish of Farnham in Surrey, he had an intimate knowledge of country life. As a youth he ran away from home and ultimately joined the army, in which he won promotion. He left it, however, to expose a financial scandal; but when he found that his evidence was likely to do more harm to himself than to the offenders, he left the country. He found his way to America, and there served his apprenticeship to the art of pamphleteering in attacking the party which sympathized with the French Revolution and in defending British institutions. For Cobbett was then a Tory, and his famous *Political Register*, which he founded in 1802 after his return to England, took the extreme

Tory side. But before the end of the war it was a violent anti-government publication, Cobbett himself suffering imprisonment for his attack on the methods employed in suppressing a disturbance which broke out among the local militia at Ely. After his release from Newgate in July 1812 he did not attract the attention which he would have liked, and he found the *Register* was declining in popularity. The experiences of 1815 and 1816, however, changed the public attitude towards him.

Cobbett was the most popular journalist of the nineteenth century. He had an unrivalled mastery of English prose coupled with a remarkable facility for feeling and arousing indignation against injustice. Egotistical and often perverse, he had the instinct for appealing to the emotions of masses of men. In November, 1816, he took the important step of issuing a cheap edition of the *Register* at twopence, avoiding the duty by omitting news and confining himself to articles. At the same time he made a strong appeal to workmen to avoid acts of violence, particularly the destruction of machinery. He drew their attention to the excessive burden of taxation and the evils of inconvertible paper money, declaring that the root cause of their misfortune was " the want of parliamentary reform." A contemporary witness, Samuel Bamford, the Lancashire weaver, says that Cobbett's writings were read in nearly every cottage in the manufacturing districts of South Lancashire, Leicester, Derby, and Nottingham. " Their influence," he writes, " was splendidly visible : he directed his readers to the true cause of their sufferings—misgovernment, and to its proper corrective—parliamentary reform. Riots soon became scarce, and from that time they have never obtained their ancient vogue with the labourers of this country."[1]

It is a curious comment on the short-sightedness of men that Cobbett's advocacy of political reform aroused more alarm than the recommendations which Robert Owen (1771–1858) brought forward as a remedy for the social problem. In 1816 Owen was drawing up a report on the steps which might be taken to meet the urgent question of unemployment. He had been requested to do so by a committee appointed by the Association for the Relief of the Manufacturing and Labouring Poor. At the moment Owen's reputation was deservedly high. He was one of the self-made men of the Industrial Revolution. Leaving his birthplace, Newtown in Montgomeryshire, at the age of ten, he had served an apprenticeship as a draper's assistant, and, after a short period of employment in a London shop, he secured a post in Manchester. With a little capital saved from a salary of £40 a year he entered into partnership with a fellow-Welshman to make Crompton's mules for the cotton industry. He was so successful that he applied for and obtained a good post as manager of a cotton factory when he was twenty. His achievement in spinning fine yarn suitable for making muslins attracted attention, and he became one of the managing directors of the Chorlton Twist Company. In the course of business he visited Glasgow, and through a mutual acquaintance was introduced to his future wife, Caroline Dale, the daughter of David Dale, then one of the most prominent citizens. He visited the mills at New Lanark, and learning that Dale wished

[1] Bamford, *Passages in the Life of a Radical*, p. 6. Bamford (1788–1872) was at the head of the Middleton people at Peterloo. John Bright wrote his epitaph: "Bamford was a Reformer when to be so was unsafe, and he suffered for his faith."

to dispose of them bought them for himself and his partners. But from the day he undertook the management of New Lanark Owen showed that he had a far greater ambition than that of personal advancement. He was determined to conduct a social experiment. The conditions were sufficiently discouraging. There were between 1800 and 2000 workpeople, including some 500 parish children; they were addicted to petty theft and drunkenness. Owen, however, conquered their natural suspicion of his designs. By his simplicity of character and genuine benevolence he established a paternal rule. He began by making dishonesty and drunkenness difficult, but resolutely refused to resort to punishment. Cleanliness and good order were insisted upon in the mills, the streets, and even in the houses. A village store was established where the workpeople could buy their goods at a fair price and the profits were expended on education. He raised the age at which children were employed to ten, and provided schools not only for children between five and ten but also for infants. Experiments were made in reducing the hours of labour and providing recreation. Owen's work at New Lanark attracted considerable attention. There was a continual stream of visitors, including representatives of most European countries. A recent writer, with pardonable enthusiasm, declares: "His rules for New Lanark deserve to be commemorated, for the last hundred years have been spent in securing for everybody what Owen secured for his workpeople at once."[1]

Owen's proposals for meeting the problem of unemployment were partly suggested by his experience at New Lanark. But he did not confine himself to a few practical suggestions. He elaborated a

[1] F. S. Marvin, *The Century of Hope*, p. 88.

general scheme out of which sprang his later teaching on socialism and co-operation. The unemployed were to live in self-sufficing communities, of from 500 to 1500, housed in a quadrangular building and cultivating the adjacent land. The plan was welcomed in the *Times* as an alternative to the system of poor relief, but some doubt was expressed about the cost it would involve. Owen, however, already had a vision of a New Moral World. The horrors of the factory system were to be abolished. Men and women were to live in these "villages of co-operation," where not merely production of commodities but also education and cultured leisure would be possible. He saw no reason why the happiness of mankind, as he conceived it, should be sacrificed to the making of profits for the classes he considered to be unproductive.

Owen's remedy for the distress of the period is in marked contrast with Cobbett's. Owen had no faith in political action. In the one instance in which he invoked it he was deeply disappointed by the result. He conducted a tour round the factories in England and Scotland in order to accumulate evidence to strengthen the case for legislation, and he was the most important witness examined by Peel's Committee on the employment of children in factories. The subsequent Factory Act of 1819—the first real Factory Act—modified every suggestion Owen had made. He wished to prohibit the employment of children under ten; the Act placed the limit at nine. Owen recommended that no person under eighteen should be employed for more than 10½ hours a day, exclusive of meal-times; the Act provided that no person under sixteen should be employed for more than 12 hours, exclusive of meal-times. Owen would have applied the Act to textile mills other than cotton; the Act was limited to cotton mills. An even more important modification was the rejection of Owen's advice that paid and qualified inspectors should be appointed to administer the Act. Inspection remained in the hands of the local justices of the peace. Owen had no faculty for political agitation and was out of sympathy with the reform movement. His teaching became more prophetic. The days of the Old Immoral World seemed numbered and mankind was on the eve of a new era. Consequently he had little or no interest in tampering with the institutions on which the seal of doom was already set. He deprecated all violence. The transition to the new age was apparently to be a peaceful one. As far as he would approve of action it was to be industrial rather than political. Cobbett believed that a political democracy would eradicate the abuses of his day: Owen looked to an industrial democracy in which political machinery would be relatively unimportant.

The violence of Cobbett and the Utopianism of Owen long contributed to obscure the importance of their respective contributions to the formation of working-class opinion. Much more justice has always been paid to the influence of the school of thought which owes its economics to Adam Smith and its political principles to Jeremy Bentham. The explanation is simple. They had a definite body of doctrine based on a few intelligible principles and yielding practical guidance in the promotion of reform. The implications of these principles were explored with the persistency of genius by Bentham himself. And he founded a school of disciples, who combined devotion to himself with remarkable personal qualities of their own. In a very real sense they were working with the grain of society. Their teaching, or a perversion of it, corresponded with the interests of influential sections of the community. Adam Smith had insisted on the desirability of allowing free play to individual initiative. He had shown in more than one instance the stupidity of governmental control. But the elaboration of the doctrine of *laissez-faire* was due to Bentham. Starting from the hypothesis that the end of legislation was the promotion of the greatest happiness of the greatest number, he subjected the whole body of English law to a searching analysis. His work, however, was essentially constructive. He possessed to a remarkable degree the ability to build on the foundations he had laid down. For sixty years he was indefatigable in pursuing his studies and, although himself a recluse, he came to exercise a determining influence on political development. The political and economic teaching comprehended by the term *laissez-faire* was never entirely unchallenged, but for a considerable time its prestige placed it beyond any effective criticism. It became an orthodoxy which it was impious to assail. Like other orthodoxies it had served its purpose before it obtained that position.

As an exponent of *laissez-faire* or Individualism no better example could be chosen than Francis Place (1771-1854). He came to occupy a unique position among the disciples of Jeremy Bentham, for he was more closely associated with the working-class movements of the day than any of the others. Born a Londoner, the son of the keeper of a private debtors' prison, Francis Place had an irregular education in a variety of schools supplemented by an intimate knowledge of the unruly street life of the time. When he resisted his father's proposal that he should become a lawyer, that worthy (now a public-house keeper) handed him over to one of his customers to teach him the trade of leather-breeches making. He married when he was nineteen, and, owing to disputes in his trade, experienced all the misery of prolonged unemployment. By dint of great perseverance he ultimately built up a good business for himself at Charing Cross and then threw himself into public affairs. He collected a library of books and pamphlets, and his invaluable stock of information on industrial matters was always at the disposal of reformers. Place, however, avoided taking a public part himself, preferring to achieve his ends through others. He was personally acquainted with all the leaders of the new schools of thought. When Cobbett had been prosecuted for his article in the *Register* Place assisted him in his defence. That experience finally estranged them. Place had no sympathy with Cobbett's violence of language and thought him lacking in any consistent principles. He was also too sceptical to accept Robert Owen's views of the impending transformation of society, though he was profoundly impressed by his possession of " an imperturbable temper and an enthusiastic desire to promote the happiness of mankind." By temperament Place had a much stronger attraction towards the Benthamites. He had got to know James Mill in 1808, and through him he was eventually introduced to the Master himself in 1812.[1] In the course

[1] These introductions were difficult to arrange. Robert Owen in his *Autobiography* gives his own experience: " After some preliminary communication with our mutual friends, James Mill and Francis Place, his then two chief counsellors, and some correspondence between him and myself, it was at length arrived at that I was to come to his hermit-like retreat at a particular hour, and that I was, upon entering, to proceed upstairs. I pursued these instructions, and he, in great trepidation, met me, and taking my hand, while his whole frame was agitated with excitement, he hastily said, ' Well, well ! It is all over. We are introduced. Come into my study.' " Bentham agreed to become a partner in the New Lanark Mills. Owen was indeed highly favoured. When Madame de Staël wrote to one

of the following years a close intimacy grew up between them. Place owed his grounding in principles to his friendship with Mill and Bentham; he repaid the debt by keeping them in touch with the actual occurrences in the world outside.

Place's most remarkable single achievement was the repeal of the Combination Laws. It was a task which needed knowledge, conviction, and management. His grasp of the question in all its intricacies was complete. He had himself been the secretary of more than one trade club, and he had suffered the consequences as a black-listed journeyman who, in despair of finding employment again at his trade, had been on the point of becoming a scavenger. For years he had interested himself in every trade dispute and had collected a mass of information to which he gave publicity whenever opportunity offered itself. The Combination Laws were condemned by his Individualist principles. He believed that each person was the best judge of his own interests, and no legislative enactment should prevent him from pursuing it. The workmen had shown that they wished to combine, and the courts had savagely punished them for doing so. Curiously enough, Place thought the existence of the Laws promoted combinations by provoking defensive measures. In a letter to Sir Francis Burdett he writes: " Combinations will soon cease to exist. Men have been kept together for long periods only by the oppression of the laws; these being repealed, combinations will lose the matter which cements them into masses, and they will fall to pieces. All will be as orderly as even a Quaker

of Bentham's secretaries to arrange an interview for her, adding, " Tell Bentham I will see nobody till I have seen him," the Master's reply was, "Sorry for it, for then she will never see anybody."

could desire. He knows nothing of the working people who can suppose that, when left at liberty to act for themselves, without being driven into permanent associations by the oppression of the laws, they will continue to contribute money for distant and doubtful experiments, for uncertain and precarious benefits." This is perhaps a sound deduction from Individualist principles: it is an unfortunate forecast of the future of combinations. His unrivalled skill in political management, however, is revealed in the manner in which the repeal was effected. Through Joseph Hume (1777–1855), a Radical member of the House of Commons, a Select Committee was secured in February 1824. Hume was appointed chairman. The working-class witnesses were all privately examined by Place and their evidence arranged for the Committee. The recommendations of the Committee were thrown into the form of resolutions; for it was feared that a report would invite discussion. The Bills based on the resolutions passed through the House without attracting attention, care having been taken to induce certain members not to speak on them. Place also succeeded in anticipating any opposition in the House of Lords. His triumph, however, was jeopardized by an almost immediate outbreak of industrial troubles. He had not calculated on this, and he exerted himself by letters to individuals and to provincial papers to prevent strikes. The employers were now thoroughly alarmed and, for their part, demanded the re-enactment of the Combination Laws. Representatives of the Glasgow cotton manufacturers and the Thames shipbuilders approached the Ministry and won the ear of Peel and Huskisson. A new committee of inquiry was appointed. Hume and Place pressed upon its attention delegates from all parts of the county who desired to give evidence. By skilful manipulation the situation was saved. The new Act of 1825 followed that of the previous year in repealing the Combination Laws; but the possible activities of a trade combination were strictly limited by the common law of conspiracy, which might be invoked if workmen in the conduct of a strike interfered with the free action of others. This qualification, although it was not contemplated in 1824, was strictly in accord with Individualist opinion. Place wanted to enlarge the sphere of free contract. He thought that the repeal of the Combination Laws would achieve this purpose and then combination would cease to offer any attractions to workmen. If, however, they continued to form combinations and proceeded to interfere with the interests of employers, and of workmen who did not wish to join them, a problem emerged for which the Individualists had no solution. There would be a clash of interests in which the liberty of one or other would be endangered.

To return to political reform. The opposition of the two parties was wearing down. The Tories were suffering from dissension within their own ranks. The group associated with Canning adopted a more liberal foreign policy, and Huskisson had considerably modified trade policy, making a breach in strict protection. The Duke of Wellington had been forced to yield on the question of Catholic Emancipation. The Whig leaders, on the other hand, were coming under the influence of the Radicals. Bentham had realized that his plans for legal reform required a preliminary constitutional reform. He had promulgated a scheme for a wide extension of the suffrage, the secret ballot, annual parliaments, and equal electoral districts in 1809.

The arguments of the Individualists secured an intellectual assent among those who were simply alienated by Cobbett's method of conducting reform propaganda. Revolution on the Continent had its reactions in England. In 1830 France dethroned the king she had been forced to accept after her defeat in 1815. In the same year Belgium asserted her independence of Holland. Earl Grey, the leader of the Whigs, was personally committed to reform, and formed his first Ministry in November. The first Reform Bill led to Grey's defeat, the dissolution of Parliament, and another General Election. The reformers were again returned and the second Reform Bill introduced on 24 November, 1831. It was rejected by the House of Lords. There were wild protests in different parts of the country and a riot of three days' duration in Bristol, where great damage was done. After a prorogation the third Reform Bill was introduced in December, and, as it encountered opposition in the Lords, the Ministry resigned. The Duke of Wellington made a vain attempt to form a Tory Ministry. Preparations were made to resort to force if necessary, and Francis Place struck upon the plan of stimulating a run on the Bank of England by issuing a placard, "To stop the Duke, go for gold." The King had to agree to the Whig demand for permission to create peers in order to overcome the opposition in the Lords. The threat secured the passage of the Bill.

The Reform Act of 1832 must be judged by remembering what it superseded. It disfranchised 57 boroughs and reduced the membership of 30 others to one each. This was regarded as a great inroad upon the rights of property, and in effect it deprived a comparatively small group of a strong hold on the House of Commons. The Constitution which had been held up as the perfect expression of the wisdom of our ancestors suffered drastic amendment. The counties received 62 additional seats, and 63 were ascribed to cities and boroughs hitherto unrepresented. By this means the old anomalies were swept away. Representation was based on some intelligible principle. The case for further reform, when circumstances demanded it, was granted. For there was nothing sacrosanct about the Reform Act. The franchise still remained restricted. In the counties, copyholders, leaseholders for lives, and tenants at will, paying over £50 a year, were added to the old 40s. freeholders; in the boroughs, the vote was given to £10 householders, thus actually disfranchising working men in such constituencies as that of Westminster, which had a wide franchise prior to 1832. The Act admitted the middle class to full political power. It made the House of Commons a representative body, but representative of a minority.

Reform of Parliament was necessarily followed by reform of local government. A Royal Commission was appointed in 1833. It consisted of a score of young barristers whose opinions were distinctly Benthamite; John Blackburne was chairman and Joseph Parkes secretary. They found that "the existing Municipal Corporations neither possess nor deserve the confidence or respect of Your Majesty's subjects, and that a thorough reform must be effected before they can become . . . useful and efficient instruments of local government." In the 237 towns they examined there were twenty-two ways of acquiring the freedom, i.e. the right of citizenship. Often the freemen were a mere handful, e.g. Portsmouth with a population of 46,000 had 102 freemen. In 186 boroughs the councils were self-elected. The Corporations, for the most part, neglected the public duties, such as the supervision of building and the supply of the communal services, such as water, street lighting, and even drainage. The report of the Royal Commission was in favour of popularly elected bodies with power to levy rates and responsible for general administration. Its recommendations were pressed upon the Whigs by the Radical group, and found expression in the Municipal Corporations Act (1835). The representative principle had won another victory.

CHAPTER IV

DISILLUSIONMENT

THE Reform Bill was carried by a temporary alliance of the Whigs with Radical opinion throughout the country. In London and the industrial centres the Radicals supplied the driving force, and, during the critical days when the Duke of Wellington was trying to construct a Ministry, they made preparations for a general rising in support of the Bill. The initiative was to be taken by Birmingham. There Thomas Attwood was the leader of the Political Union of the Middle and Lower Classes, and, in the opinion of Place, "the most influential man in England." He certainly wielded great power at this juncture, though his proposal to assemble a million men on Hampstead Heath would probably have overtaxed his resources. It must not be supposed, however, that the Radicals had the working class solidly behind them. There grew up in the course of the contest a very formidable opposition to the Bill, particularly among the advanced section of working men in London and Lancashire. The centre of this opposition in London was the National Union of the Working Classes and Others, which was founded in April 1831. It was the successor of a number of short-lived organizations which had been formed by the disciples of Robert Owen. The leading members did not share Owen's antipathy towards political reform. They had learnt from Cobbett and Hunt to believe in the vote, but their conception of the use they would make of it they owed to Owen's socialist teaching. Electoral reform was but a step towards social reconstruction. Their attitude towards the Reform Bill is intelligible enough. In their opinion it was more likely to impede than to assist them in the attainment of their ends. Political power would be given to the very class which had profited from the Industrial Revolution—a class to which, according to the analysis of society which they accepted, they were necessarily opposed. In short, they objected to the general enfranchisement of their employers. The same opinion was apparently held among the textile workers of Lancashire, for their leader, John Doherty, told Francis Place in October, 1831, that the people ought no longer to be shuffled off with a Bill which could do them no good.

The National Union put forward in November, 1841, a declaration which reveals its debt to the doctrines of the French Revolution on the one hand, and is an interesting anticipation of Chartism on the other. All men, they stated, are born free and equal, and possess a number of rights natural and inalienable. Among these is the right to the whole product of their labour. This is a reference to a theory which was taught by Thomas Hodgskin (1783–1869), and exercised a profound influence on working opinion long before it was taken up and elaborated by Karl Marx. Hodgskin had been a naval lieutenant, but, after attacking the system of impressment, was dismissed the service, and turned to journalism, James Mill securing him a post as reporter to the *Morning Chronicle*. He assisted in the foundation of the London Mechanics Institute, and, in spite of opposition of Francis Place—who liked him personally but disapproved of his ideas —he was appointed Lecturer in Political Economy. There his teaching was imbibed by men who were destined to play an important part in the Chartist movement, particularly Lovett and Hetherington. In 1825 he had published his *Labour Defended against the Claims of Capital, or the Unproductiveness of Capital Proved, with reference to the Present Combinations amongst Journeymen.* His tract, as the title indicates, attempted to answer questions which had arisen in the course of the struggle for the repeal of the Combination Laws. Much had been said about the necessity of protecting capital, and constant appeal had been made to the teaching of the political economists in support of the contentions of the employers. Hodgskin had studied the works of Adam Smith and David Ricardo.[1] From the argument of the latter he derived his distinctive doctrine. The economists distinguished three factors of production, Land, Labour, and Capital, each with its appropriate functions and rewards. The share of the possessors of Land was rent, of Labour, wages, and of Capital, profits. On what principles is the distribution made? Ricardo explains that rent is a payment for the use of the "original and indestructible powers of the soil." The labourer must receive enough for subsistence for himself and his family. The remainder, a very considerable proportion of the whole, goes to capitalists. Hodgskin denies that capital has any legitimate claim to this share. He refers to Ricardo's own statement of the

[1] "It was Ricardo, not (Robert) Owen, who gave the really effective inspiration to English socialism. That inspiration was indirect and negative, but it is unmistakable" (Professor Foxwell's Introduction to Menger's *Right to the Whole Produce of Labour*, p. lxxxiii). Hodgskin's deductions from Ricardo's premises illustrate how the anti-capitalistic economics originated.

"relative quantity of labour as almost exclusively determining the relative values of commodities." Against the theory that capital must be paid because it is an accumulation which its possessors put at the disposal of the labourers, he argues that there is no such store; labourers are enabled to work because other groups of labourers are concurrently producing what they require. The capitalist insinuates himself between these groups and appropriates a large share of their products for his own ends. This is the cause of poverty. The remedy is to recognize that labour is the source and measure of value. The National Union therefore had a belief in universal suffrage, an economic theory which they opposed to the orthodox teaching, and a social revolutionary purpose. Place knew that if their opinions infected the rank and file of the working men the Whigs would draw back from the Reform proposals. He had therefore to contrive, since he was personally convinced of the desirability of the Reform Bill as a distinct step towards a wider franchise, to rally to the support of the Radicals a sufficiently impressive number of working men. So he created the National Political Union at the end of October, 1831, in the face of the opposition of the extremists. Through this organization he was able to maintain during the critical days in the following year a strong agitation in favour of the Bill. He managed to prevent any serious outbreak, while impressing upon the Government the probable consequences of not proceeding with the Bill. But the passing of the Bill changed the situation. The opponents of the measure, which they held would damage the interests of the working class, could now point to the enactments of the new Parliament in support of their contention. The Radicals themselves had to recognize that there was no disposition to take any further steps towards the realization of democracy. Consequently the schism of 1832 was eventually healed, and the extremists came to exercise a strong influence over working-class opinion. The renewed movement in favour of reform did not begin to exercise its full pressure until 1836. In the meanwhile, the reaction against industrialism had revealed itself in two important movements: a revolutionary phase of trade unionism, and a humanitarian protest against factory conditions.

The trades union movement was essentially an attempt to achieve the inclusion of all workers in one great organization. The first step was taken by the textile operatives of Lancashire and Yorkshire. They formed in 1829 the Grand General Union of the United Kingdom. Experience had shown that local unions could not successfully resist a combination of employers. The new organization, therefore, was to unite the operatives of England, Scotland, and Ireland. John Doherty, the leader of the Manchester cotton-spinners, was appointed general secretary. He was an Irishman who, after working as a boy in the cotton-mills at Larne, migrated to Manchester in 1816. In 1825 he had given strong support to the agitation against the re-enactment of the Combination Laws. It has already been mentioned that he was not impressed by the Reform Bill. The explanation is, that from the beginning of the trades union movement he had been working for a social revolution. The Grand General Union gave place to his much more ambitious National Association for the Protection of Labour which was formed in 1830. Doherty soon secured nearly 150 separate unions as members of this trades union, and while textile unions still predominated, other societies also joined. In 1831 the National Association began to publish a weekly paper called the *Voice of the People,* the object of which was "to unite the productive classes of the community in one common bond of union." Although it cost sevenpence a week, the paper is said to have attained a circulation of 30,000 copies. For a variety of reasons the National Association failed to maintain the position it had gained. The idea of a trades union, however, soon found new expression in the Builders' Union or the General Trades Union which comprehended all the trades employed in building. It had an elaborate constitution, and a ritual which included the administration of oaths of secrecy and obedience. Their attitude towards the employers provoked retaliation, which took the form of "presenting the document," that is, of requiring that each applicant for work should formally repudiate the union. Robert Owen spoke at its annual delegate meeting held at Manchester in September, 1833. He told them that if the productive classes would enter into a universal compact they could retain in their own hands the whole wealth of the community, because "labour is the source of all wealth." Owen now threw himself with his wonted energy into the working out of the trades union ideal. He formed the Grand National Consolidated Trades Union, which marks the culmination of the movement. Lodges of this union sprang up all over the country, in many cases including in their membership women workers and farm labourers. The numbers appear to have reached half a million in a few months. Such an organization was quite unmanageable, for, while all the members had general grievances on which Owen proposed to base a common policy, they were constantly preoccupied with their particular complaints. The employers continued to present the document, and, when the men refused to sign, they locked them out; 1500, for instance, were locked out on this ground at Derby. The union did not have sufficient financial resources to meet these expenses. In March, 1834, it came into conflict with the law. Six labourers of the village of Tolpuddle, in Dorsetshire, were accused of administering an oath to new members of a local lodge. They were found guilty, and sentenced to seven years' transportation. This savage sentence aroused great indignation among working men. The Grand National organized protest meetings all over the country, and a trade union demonstration was arranged in London. But as the upper classes, who had been genuinely scared by the growth of trades unionism, generally approved of strong action, the Government was able to resist the pressure of working-class opinion. The conviction of the Dorchester labourers strengthened the general policy of the union for the moment, but unsuccessful strikes and internal difficulties undermined it before the autumn of 1834, and it collapsed. Direct industrial action had hopelessly failed. On the other hand, it is true that political agitation had achieved a doubtful victory in 1832. Owen's followers, however, had always been torn between loyalty to him and a desire to achieve political democracy. Their political tendencies now became more pronounced, and their belief that universal suffrage was a necessary preliminary to social reconstruction led them into the Chartist movement.

The humanitarian protest against factory conditions also contributed to the same tendency; but it introduced a new element. The leaders, Michael Thomas Sadler, Richard Oastler, Joseph Rayner Stephens, and Antony Ashley Cooper, were all Tories. Sadler (1780–1835) had opposed Catholic

Emancipation and the Reform Bill; Oastler (1789–1861) was a Churchman and a Protectionist; Lord Ashley (1801–85),[1] who was a generation younger, was opposed to Catholic Emancipation and in favour of Protection. Stephens (1805–79) had entered the Wesleyan ministry when he was twenty, and, after a few years of mission work in Sweden, returned in 1830 to a church at Ashton-under-Lyne. His opinions, and perhaps even more his energy in giving expression to them, led to his withdrawal from the Connexion. In his subsequent career he displayed the strength and weakness of the revivalist preacher. He stirred his audiences by violent denunciation supported by appeals to the Hebrew prophets, and his ascendancy over the advanced movements among the working class was unchallenged in the North. His weakness was his recklessness in making assertions and his impatience of any critical examination of the facts. Richard Oastler was a kindred spirit. He was the steward of an estate near Huddersfield. In 1830 he attracted widespread attention by writing a series of letters to the *Leeds Mercury* on "Slavery in Yorkshire." He was moved to take this step by hearing a number of speeches at an Anti-Slavery meeting at Leeds, in which it was maintained that it was the pride of Britain that a slave could not exist on her soil. He invited the reformers to examine conditions much nearer home than the West Indies: "Thousands of our fellow-creatures and fellow-subjects, both male and female, the inhabitants of a Yorkshire town, are at this very moment existing in a state of slavery more horrid

[1] Antony Ashley Cooper was known as Lord Ashley from 1811 to 1851, when he succeeded to the title of Earl of Shaftesbury, by which he is now generally referred to even for the earlier period.

than are the victims of that hellish system—colonial slavery." Why should not the children working in the worsted mills be protected by similar enactments as those applied to cotton factories ? The agitation which he launched was extraordinarily successful in Yorkshire, where he became " the king " of factory reformers. He naturally attracted the attention of Robert Owen, and also lent his support to Sadler, who represented a Yorkshire constituency in Parliament. In 1831 Sadler introduced a Ten Hours Bill, on the second reading of which he made a speech contesting the view that there was any real freedom of contract between employer and employed. He showed that normally the two parties to the wages contract did not meet on equal terms, and consequently all deductions based on the assumption that they did were false. The opposition to the Bill was so strong that Sadler had to be content with the appointment of a Select Committee. In collecting evidence for this Committee, over which he presided, he undermined his health. He was defeated in the election of 1832 by Macaulay. A new parliamentary leader was discovered in Lord Ashley. Although the report of the Sadler Committee was set aside, a new inquiry proved that legislation was desirable. Consequently the Act of 1833 was passed. Its importance is threefold: (1) It was made applicable to woollen, worsted, hemp, flax, tow, linen, and silk mills as well as to cotton, i.e., all the textiles were covered; (2) it made special provision for " young persons " as well as children ; no one under eighteen was to do night-work or more than twelve hours a day, or a total of sixty-nine a week; the hours of children between nine and thirteen were specially limited; (3) it provided for the appointment of four Government inspectors with power to enter any factory, examine conditions, call witnesses and summon any person to give evidence. The establishment of special officials to see that the Act was enforced marks a new stage in the history of factory legislation.

The Act of 1833 did not satisfy the reformers in the North. Sadler's Bill provided for a ten hours' day for all under eighteen, and had been enthusiastically supported by popular meetings in Yorkshire and Lancashire. Oastler demanded that the age should be raised to twenty-one. When the 1833 Government Bill was before Parliament a meeting of between a hundred and a hundred and fifty thousand at Bradford protested against any modification of the ten hours' principle. There were threats that the passage of the Bill would be the signal for a general strike. The Ten Hours movement, organized by local short-time committees, continued to press for legislation until the claim was recognized in the Ten Hours Act of 1847.

From 1836 the popular movement in the North was directed against the Poor Law Amendment Act of 1834. It raised issues which exactly suited Stephens' controversial methods, for the opposition to its principles combined the practical and the sentimental. A Royal Commission had been appointed in 1832 to report on the administration of poor relief. The Report which it presented in 1834 was largely the work of Edwin Chadwick (1800–90), a young disciple of Jeremy Bentham, and Nassau Senior (1790–1864), an orthodox political economist. It is therefore a purely Individualist document in its analysis of existing abuses and in its recommendations for reform. The main problem with which the Commissioners were faced was that of able-bodied pauperism, particularly in rural parishes. The Speenhamland system of giving relief in aid of wages had become normal. To eradicate this evil the Commissioners recommended the adoption of the principle that the position of the able-bodied pauper should be less eligible than that of the independent labourer of the lowest class. Their method of applying the principle of "less eligibility" was the workhouse test, which they considered would prove to be self-acting. An able-bodied applicant for poor relief would be required to show that he was a genuine case by entering the workhouse, where he would be under restraint and discipline and his diet would be inferior to that of the lowest paid independent labourer. This test would operate, it was supposed, to force the applicant to exhaust every possible effort to find work before applying for admission to the workhouse. In order to provide workhouses parishes were thrown together to form unions and the local administration was entrusted to elected Boards of Guardians. General uniformity of administration was to be secured by a central authority enjoying extensive powers. At first this duty was entrusted to Poor Law Commissioners (1834–47), three experts of whom Sir George Nicholls is the best known. The obvious criticism of these recommendations is that they are too neatly compact for practical application. On paper they are logical, precise, and complete; but the administrators who tried to apply them would find their material intractable and their efforts characterized as inhuman. This is exactly what happened. The Poor Law Amendment Act of 1834 was based in the main on the Report. The three Poor Law Commissioners proceeded to put the law into operation as speedily as workhouses could be provided. It may be doubted whether any bureaucrats ever had such abuse poured on their heads as the "three kings of Somerset House." J. R. Stephens stirred his audiences to fever heat. "If the cottage is not permitted," he concluded one of his perorations, "to be the abode of man and wife, and if the smiling infant is to be dragged from a father's arms and a mother's bosom, it is because these hell-hounds of Commissioners have set up the command of their master the devil, against our God."

There were others who drew more temperate, though not less significant, conclusions from the passing of the Poor Law Amendment Act. They pointed out that it was a complete demonstration of the fact that the reformed Parliament represented the employers' interests. The effect of the law was to promote mobility of labour by depriving the workman of the assistance which he could claim from his parish. In the past he had been able to tide over a period of high prices, for his wages were made up to a certain amount assessed on the basis of the price of bread. That security was now gone. He had to leave his parish to seek employment in the new industrial areas where fluctations, owing to the very nature of large-scale industry, were more frequent and more acute. Moreover, he found that he had to compete with hundreds of his fellows for employment, a fact which accentuated his sense of insecurity and tended to provide the employers with cheap labour. But this feeling also produced a class consciousness. These masses were material for Chartist propaganda; the speakers found in denouncing the new Poor Law they provoked a ready response, for it was a grievance very generally experienced and always bitterly resented.

The opposition to the Poor Law Amendment

Act first clearly brought out the essential difference of point of view between the Benthamites and the working-class organizations. Francis Place knew the authors of the Poor Law Report and fully approved of their recommendations. He was not without hope that he would be nominated one of the three Commissioners; an office which, he declares in a private letter, he would discharge "with all my heart and soul . . . utterly careless of the abuse which will be showered down in all possible forms on the obnoxious Commissioners."[1] When he assisted later in drawing up the People's Charter he particularly asked that the movement should not condemn the new Poor Law. Cobbett, on the other hand, never suffered theoretical principles to harden his heart. He had been returned for Oldham in 1832 and was one of the few members of the House of Commons who opposed the Poor Law Amendment Bill. He followed this up by writing his *Legacy to Labourers*, a pamphlet in which he developed his case against the proposals. It was based on his view of the Protestant Reformation. In the Middle Ages the Church, which held land in trust for the purpose, dispensed charity to those in want. This land was seized by the gentry in the sixteenth century still burdened with the obligation to provide for the poor, a fact which was legally recognized by the Poor Law of 1601. From that date the poor had enjoyed the right to assistance from a fund raised by assessments levied on the receivers of rent. The Act of 1834, however, deprived them of this right without any compensation. Oastler followed up this line of argument, maintaining that, since the poor had been robbed of their legal rights, they should retaliate by refusing to pay landlords their rents. In his

[1] Wallas, *Life of Place*, p. 332.

mind the question of the Poor Law Amendment Act was closely associated with that of the Ten Hours' Day, for the limitation of the hours of labour, if it could be effected, would do something to counteract the competition for employment which the Act was intended to promote.

The experience of the years 1837 to 1843 gave coherence to this general body of criticism. In the elections of 1837 very few Radicals had been able to retain their seats, and the Whig leader, Lord John Russell, announced that it was not the time to reopen the Reform question. This view of "Finality Jack"—as Russell was nicknamed—demonstrated that the Whigs were satisfied with the Reform Act of 1832, and the advantages which the enfranchised middle class derived from it. The breach with the reformers was complete. Francis Place, it must be remembered, was part author of the People's Charter. These political events coincided with a serious financial crisis which began in the United States of America and soon extended to Great Britain. It was first felt in Lancashire, where the Northern and Central Bank of Manchester was in difficulties owing to its American investments. The shock to the industrial world was immediately marked by a rise in prices of raw material. Adjustment was prevented by a series of bad harvests at home, beginning in 1838, which prolonged the depression of the markets. The fall in wages was accentuated by a rise in prices, which was due to the shortage of necessaries. In these circumstances the effect of the Poor Law Amendment Act was brought home to those who were out of employment or otherwise unable to maintain their standard of life. The criticism of the Factory system on the ground that it undermined their power of resistance and deprived them of all security, won general approval among working men. Opposition to the Corn Laws was also revived, and the way prepared for the great agitation of the next decade. As a remedy, or rather as a means towards a remedy, the People's Charter was promulgated.

CHAPTER V

CROSS-CURRENTS

THE People's Charter was a document thrown into the form of a Parliamentary Bill which provided for (1) Universal Suffrage, (2) Equal Electoral Districts, (3) Voting by Ballot, (4) Annual Parliaments, (5) Removal of Property Qualification for Parliamentary Candidates, and (6) Payment of Members. The Charter was drafted by William Lovett with the assistance of Francis Place, and circulated to democratic organizations throughout the country in the summer of 1838 by the London Working Men's Association. Chartism, however, is much older than the Charter, and much more comprehensive than its six points. The political programme can be traced back half a century to the beginnings of what came to be known as Radicalism. On the surface, therefore, Chartism was only a new appeal to the spirit of reform; a reassertion of the belief in political democracy. It was, it may be said, the third appeal to these principles which had been made since the end of the Napoleonic War. In the years of distress which had immediately followed Waterloo, reform had been advocated by Cobbett and Hunt as a remedy for the evils which arose from unemployment and the results of the adoption of machinery. That movement was temporarily suppressed by the action of the Government. But there was a revival in the later 'twenties which led to an alliance between the Whigs and the Radicals in favour of a limited measure of reform. In the years 1830 to 1832 popular enthusiasm supported the Reform Bill, although the more thoroughgoing democrats had their misgivings about the consequence of enfranchising the middle class. Their fears were, on the whole, justified by the event. It may be said that 1834 was the test year. The Reformed Parliament approved of the Government's severity towards the trades union movement, and it also passed the Poor Law Amendment Act. The suspicion that a Parliament elected on the principles of 1832 would act in the interests of the employers was confirmed. Consequently, it seemed that the only way of escape was to reopen the question of political democracy, and to demand that the suffrage should be so extended that such class legislation would be impossible. Stated in this way, there is nothing new about Chartism. But the six points of the Charter did not exhaust the aims of its promoters. Obviously they could only be the means of attaining other purposes. The difficulty of defining these purposes and securing general agreement within their own ranks defeated the endeavours of the ablest Chartists. On the political programme, which was merely a demand for democratic machinery of government, a great variety of organizations could be brought into line, for each flattered itself that a wider franchise would assist it to introduce its own panacea. The problem was how to maintain a concentration of effort on the attainment of the six points of the Charter, subordinating every other purpose to this end. There was no immediate prospect of seeing the Charter converted into an Act of Parliament. Every set-back, and even delay itself, would tend to divide the Chartists into constitutional and revolutionary elements. And, as a matter of fact, the enthusiasts were moved more by their vision of the social regeneration which they hoped would follow the adoption of the Charter than by the six points themselves. Francis Place, speaking from the experience of a lifetime, counselled the Working Men's Association not to speak about Socialism on their platforms or to countenance denunciation of the Poor Law. This was impossible. The whole case for the Charter was social rather than political. It was launched at a time of renewed distress when there was a passionate revolt against the industrial system even more intense and widespread than in the years 1815 to 1819. In Lancashire and Yorkshire Oastler and Stephens had already aroused the bitterest feeling against the manufacturers. No amount of management in London could curb the efforts of such agitators among such a populace as that created by the Industrial Revolution.

The London Working Men's Association was founded in June 1836. Although it did not exclude the possibility of accepting assistance from outside, it confined actual membership to working men; others were elected honorary members. Its original aims were largely educational and its methods constitutional. Information of importance to the working classes was to be collected and discussed. The conclusions were to be made public in order to assist in social improvement. One of its committees, for instance, issued a report on the composition of the House of Commons, entitled the "Rotten House of Commons," which became a handbook of the advanced reformers. It is significant as a fierce denunciation of the Reform Act of 1832. The analysis of the membership of the House showed that the working class had no representation. There was a certain opposition between representatives of landlords and manufacturers, but the report did not anticipate that their differences might have important consequences for the working class. As between these two sections the report is more favourable to the landlords than to the manufacturers. Among the members of the Association the most prominent were William Lovett, Henry Hetherington, James Watson, and John Cleave. Lovett (1800–77) was appointed secretary. Born at Newlyn in Cornwall, the posthumous child of the captain of a small trading vessel, he had been brought up by his mother, a hard-working woman of strict Methodist principles. She apprenticed him to rope-making, but in 1821 he went to London, where, after many difficulties, he was admitted into the Society of Cabinetmakers. About 1829 he came under the influence of Robert Owen, and became secretary of his British Association for Promoting Co-operative Knowledge. He was closely associated with the attempt to establish the Labour Exchange Bazaar, a scheme by which Owen intended the precious metals to be superseded as a medium of exchange by labour notes, each note to represent the amount of time expended on making an article and to be exchangeable for an article or articles made in the same number of hours. Lovett did not agree with Owen's attitude towards political action, and on more than one occasion he was irritated by what he considered his somewhat autocratic conduct. At the same time he felt a strong admiration for the work of Cobbett and Hunt as champions of the people's rights. He was one of the founders of the National Union of the Working Classes and Others, and therefore a leader of the extremist opposition to the Reform Bill against which Francis Place had to contend. Throughout his public career Lovett moved steadily towards a moderate position. He abandoned the more Utopian schemes of Owen in favour of political agitation, but when he found that the leadership was falling into the hands of demagogues he instinctively drew back. Leadership seemed to him to present such strong temptations that he minimized its importance. He had a growing conviction that education was an essential factor in social progress. With these opinions, confirmed by a modest, sensitive, and somewhat melancholy nature, Lovett was unfitted to maintain a strong personal hold over a popular agitation.

The London Working Men's Association launched the Charter but failed to control the helm. As the distress, which was caused by acute depression of trade and a succession of bad harvests, spread, the old local democratic organizations revived. Each contributed something to the Chartist movement. The Charter itself was accepted as a general battle-cry, though it never became the one object to which all others were to be subordinated. In Birmingham the Political Union which had been so active from 1830 to 1832 was refounded under the new stimulus. Thomas Attwood again took control, and put in the forefront of the campaign his monetary theory. The distress, he pointed out, was due to the restriction of the currency, and could be removed by the issue of paper money, which would increase the volume of business and eliminate unemployment. He seems to have counted that the enthusiasm for the Charter would enable him to carry through his scheme if he could tack it on to the agitation. In this he miscalculated. The Chartists were not convinced that his theories were sound, and his immediate following in Birmingham was too middle class to make co-operation with the Chartists of the North possible. The character of the movement, indeed, was decided by the attitude of the working class in Lancashire and Yorkshire. In the autumn of 1838 J. R. Stephens began to hold meetings in favour of the Charter. These meetings were often held by torchlight, and they attracted such numbers that the Government, fearing an outbreak of violence, prohibited the practice. Stephens, who called for universal suffrage or universal vengeance, defied the authorities and was arrested. But the Northern Chartists had already found a new leader in Feargus O'Connor, who had left London in the previous year and become the proprietor of the *Northern Star*, which was published at Leeds. He knew how to exploit the popular indignation aroused by the arrest of Stephens to augment his own influence. O'Connor (1794-1855) was a member of an Irish landed family, several members of which had played a prominent part in revolutionary movements in Ireland. Feargus himself had entered Trinity College, Dublin, and was a member of the Irish Bar. In 1832 he was returned as Member of Parliament for County Cork as a supporter of Daniel O'Connell, but, having quarrelled with his chief, he was deprived of his seat in 1835. While in London he came in touch with the leaders of the Working Men's Association. From the outset he seems to have had no sympathy with the moderate policy of the Association. After a quarrel between the supporters of Lovett and O'Connor a rival body was formed which attracted to itself all the extremists.

In after years the prominent Chartist leaders agreed that the ascendancy which O'Connor won over the movement was one of the chief explanations of its failure. He was undoubtedly a demagogue possessing great rhetorical powers and boundless energy. There can be no question of his popularity.

Everywhere—and O'Connor was ubiquitous—his audiences were impressed by his commanding stature, his aristocratic features, and his stentorian voice. His speeches were compounded of flattery, denunciation, humour, and racy anecdotes. The working class was suspicious of middle-class leadership, but O'Connor caused no offence by boasting of his descent from Roderic O'Connor, the twelfth-century King of all Ireland. He treated them to long narratives of the doings of his ancestors and of himself in Ireland which had at least the merit of being entertaining. Every cause of discontent he exploited to the full without any regard to a constructive programme. The *Northern Star* reflected his methods. And it was the only Chartist paper that achieved any success. O'Connor gave his readers what they wanted, recognizing that to extend circulation it is necessary to lower the tone of the Press. He used Chartism in the interests of the *Northern Star*, and his paper to secure the leadership of the movement for himself. The members of the Working Men's Association were attacked as betrayers of the interests of their fellows and friends of the middle class. As a newspaper proprietor O'Connor was able to ride down all opponents. He won the gratitude of many by giving full publicity to their speeches and adding editorial approval. But those who disagreed with him were fiercely attacked and often unscrupulously misrepresented. As a thinker O'Connor carried no weight. He borrowed from others as it suited his purpose. His chief debt seems to have been to James O'Brien, usually known as Bronterre O'Brien, on whom he bestowed the title of "the Schoolmaster of Chartism." O'Brien (1805–64) was, in fact, something of an original thinker. After graduating at Trinity

College, Dublin, he came to London to study law. In 1831 he started the *Poor Man's Guardian*, a paper which took the extremist view during the Reform Bill agitation. He knew Cobbett and Hunt intimately, and was convinced that universal suffrage was a condition precedent to social reform. It was in his opinion a mistake for Robert Owen to belittle the importance of political action, and he ventured to appeal to him to reconsider his attitude. But the co-operative or communistic aspect of Owen's teaching influenced him very strongly. In his writings the Owenite vocabulary is constantly employed. O'Brien's personal contribution to Socialist thought was the correlation of Owen's teaching with the principles of the French Revolution. He translated into English Buonarroti's account of the conspiracy of Babeuf, and also wrote an appreciative study of Robespierre as the exponent of pure democracy. Throughout the trades union movement he held that the men were ill advised to resort to strikes; political action, he argued, would be more efficacious and direct. His economic theory was based on the conception that two classes existed, the possessing and the dispossessed. Since labour alone was productive, the possessing class had by one means or another robbed the others of their rights. He strongly advocated the nationalization of land. Like O'Connor, he was admitted to honorary membership of the London Working Men's Association, but his teaching, particularly on the necessary antagonism between the classes, led him to support O'Connor and to contribute articles to the *Northern Star*.

The immediate outcome of the Chartist propaganda in the industrial centres was the nomination of the Convention or People's Parliament which assembled in London on 4 February, 1839, i.e. on the same day as Parliament itself. The delegates included Lovett, O'Connor, and O'Brien, and discussion almost at once arose between the moderates, who favoured the employment of moral force, and the extremists, who advocated physical force. The moderates were in a majority, but their opponents were full of resources which delayed the carrying out of the main purpose of the Convention—the drawing up of the National Petition which was to be presented to Parliament in favour of the Charter. It was eventually completed, and obtained some 1,200,000 signatures. Attwood, who represented Birmingham in the House of Commons, moved for a Committee of the whole House to consider the Petition on 12 July, 1839. The subsequent debate is interesting because of the intervention of Benjamin Disraeli. He traced the whole trouble back to the Reform Act of 1832, which had transferred political power to the middle class. That class, he held, was lacking in any sense of duty towards the lower orders. Formerly, the constitution had entrusted power to those who exercised it with public spirit and genuine sympathy. The Poor Law Amendment Act was quoted as a proof of his contention. It had "outraged the whole social duties of the State." With characteristic adroitness Disraeli had seized upon the political grievances of the Chartists as an argument in favour of a return to a benevolent despotism which his imagination endowed with virtues it had never possessed. Only 46 supported Attwood's motion; 235 voted against it.

The Convention replied by adopting the proposal of a General Strike which had for some years been preached by William Benbow. It was called the "National Holiday" or "Sacred Month," and its purpose was to demonstrate that labour was the only source of wealth. O'Brien, although he was in favour of using this weapon, maintained that the Convention was unable to wield it successfully. The trade unions would certainly refuse to obey the commands of the Convention, and consequently the organization of the General Strike would be impossible. Under the threat of such action the local authorities now proceeded against Chartist leaders with the full approbation of the Government. Lovett was committed to prison for twelve months for issuing a protest against the conduct of the police at Birmingham. Henry Vincent, a fellow-member of the Working Men's Association, was imprisoned at Monmouth. The idea of rescuing the latter by force is said to have provoked the Newport Rising. On the morning of 4 November some two or three thousand Welsh miners advanced on Newport under the command of John Frost, a local Chartist leader, who had been mayor of the town. The authorities had lodged a detachment of the 45th Regiment in the Westgate Hotel. They opened fire on the Chartists, killing fourteen and wounding some fifty others. Over a hundred arrests were made and the leaders were charged with high treason. This tragedy closes the first phase of Chartism. O'Connor, who had done so much to arouse the passions which had led to disaster, was absent in Ireland at this critical juncture. His conduct was certainly open to the suspicion that he did not have the courage to convert his words into action.

The discredit which had fallen on Chartism contributed to the progress of another organization which had been formed in 1838, the year in which the Charter was promulgated. The Anti-Corn Law League, like Chartism, sprang out of the distress of the time. They were almost exactly contemporaneous, often in conflict with one another, and they never united against the protection of agriculture. The explanation of the hostility between the two movements is to be found, partly in the natural rivalry of two bodies which were seeking public support at the same time, and partly in class prejudice. Opposition to the Corn Laws certainly had as honourable a record in Radical annals as the claim to the vote. At Peterloo one of the banners bore the words, "No Corn Laws," and nothing had happened in the meantime to give working men any interest in their maintenance.[1] Why, then, did the Chartist Convention unanimously adopt a resolution against the Anti-Corn Law League? Why did the more extreme Chartists make a point of breaking up the League's meetings and so winning "glorious victories" glowingly recorded in O'Connor's *Northern Star*? Largely because the League was founded by manufacturers, the class with which the northern Chartists at any rate believed they were necessarily at war. The genesis of the League was to be traced to Manchester. Both Richard Cobden and John Bright were engaged in the cotton industry. The costly propaganda of the League was paid for by subscriptions from manufacturers. Some of its most potent economic arguments were addressed to this class. It was pointed out that the British export trade had been brought to a standstill because the ports were normally closed to imported corn. Other countries were resorting to manufactures because Great Britain would not accept their surplus of food

[1] The Free Trade Hall stands in St. Peter's Fields, the scene of Peterloo. A temporary wooden structure was opened there in 1840; it gave place to a brick building in 1843. The present stone building dates from 1856.

produce in payment for manufactured goods. The supporters of the League wished to make the country the workshop of the world, and denounced the Corn Laws because they were a hindrance to their purpose. To this some of the Chartists replied that they were by no means reconciled to the industrial system and did not wish to see its ascendancy guaranteed. Others asserted that the manufacturers were anxious to reduce the price of bread because this would enable them to lower wages. Whatever may have been the economic opinions of the manufacturers as a whole, it is certain that Cobden and Bright did not anticipate that Free Trade would lead to a fall in wages. On the contrary, they argued that it would raise wages as well as cheapen food.

Cobden (1804-63) was an agitator who must have appealed very strongly to Francis Place. He was out to repeal the Corn Laws, and he refused to complicate the issue by enlarging his programme. Bright (1811-89), who, as he afterwards proved, sincerely believed in the extended suffrage, tried to induce his friend to include it in his campaign, but without success. While he concentrated all his energy on one issue, he was always anxious to secure wider support. Hence his appeal to working men in favour of cheaper bread, an appeal which certainly detached large numbers from the ranks of the Chartists from 1840 onwards. Hence, too, his campaign to prove that tenant-farmers derived little or no benefit from protection, for their rents were high and fluctuations in prices were often ruinous. He also demonstrated that the agricultural labourer was merely a low paid consumer without any interest in the maintenance of the system. The landlord stood out as the one beneficiary of the Corn Laws. A propaganda conducted with such argumentative powers, so definitely directed to one purpose, and so resourceful in the use of methods, whether lectures, conferences, debates, or even bazaars, was bound to make inroads into the ranks of Chartism, which were lacking in cohesion and rent by distracting cries and personal recriminations.

In the course of 1840 many plans were discussed for the reorganization of the Chartist movement. The result was the accentuation of the tendency towards sectional developments. There were the National Charter Association, over which O'Connor contrived to gain complete control; a Christian Chartist movement, of which Arthur O'Neill was the most prominent member; a Chartist temperance agitation led by Vincent; while Lovett, after his release from prison, devoted himself to an organization for promoting popular education. Against every form of Chartism except that to which he himself was committed O'Connor raged in the *Northern Star*. The differences between the leaders prevented any real co-operation. Within the National Charter Association O'Connor would suffer no rival. O'Brien severed his connexion with him and stood as a parliamentary candidate for Newcastle-on-Tyne, issuing an address in which he advocated the total and immediate repeal of the Corn Laws. The situation was further complicated by the action of Joseph Sturge (1793–1859), a Quaker corn-dealer of Birmingham. His main idea was to effect a reconciliation between the middle and working classes—a task for which he was peculiarly suited, for he was entirely without ulterior motives. Sturge had been interested in the Anti-Corn Law agitation, and was alarmed by the opposition which existed between its middle-class supporters and the Chartists. He therefore proposed the formation of a Complete Suffrage movement, which was to unite the two classes in a common effort to secure radical political reform, for he believed there would have to be an extension of the franchise before any progress could be made in the direction of Free Trade. His movement, however, was quite independent of the Anti-Corn Law League, though it had the support and sympathy of a considerable section of its members. The idea of promoting the co-operation of classes attracted Lovett, and even O'Brien was well disposed towards it; but O'Connor professed to believe that it was merely an artifice of the Anti-Corn Law League to detach Chartists from their faith. This was certainly unjust to Sturge, though it is true that the Complete Suffrage movement was an indication that common Radicalism was more potent than class differences. O'Connor himself came to recognize this, and began to argue in the *Northern Star* that the middle class was composed of different elements, with some of which it was quite legitimate for the working class to co-operate. He was clearly preparing for a compromise when the strikes of August, 1844, ruined the prospect of sinking class differences. As far as can be ascertained, the stoppages, which spread from Lancashire to the Clyde, the Tyne and the Midlands, were a practically unorganized protest against a reduction of wages. But it was only natural that the Chartists and the League should attempt to show that the strikes supported their contentions. Some Chartists wished to connect them with the recent rejection by the House of Commons of the Petition drawn up by the National Charter Association. The difficulty was whether they should assume any responsibility for the strikes or not. On this question O'Connor took a strong line of his own. He held that the strikes had been deliberately provoked by the Anti-Corn Law manufacturers in order to bring pressure on the Government and to divert attention from the Charter. While the League repudiated all responsibility, it found in the strikes a confirmation of its arguments that protection of agriculture was ruining industry. John Bright, whose workpeople came out, issued an address to the working men of Rochdale, in the course of which he asserted: "If every employer and workman in the kingdom were to swear on their bended knees that wages should not fall, they would still assuredly fall if the Corn Law continues. No power on earth can maintain your wages at their present rate if the Corn Law be not repealed."

The Chartists completely failed to make any capital out of the strikes. O'Connor was probably right in maintaining that they had nothing to do with the great "turn-out," but he found himself in opposition to some extremists, who thought they now saw an opportunity of realizing the plan of a National Holiday. At the same time, his attempt to attach the opprobrium to the Anti-Corn Law League renewed the antagonism between them and the Chartists. Consequently, the prospects of a union of classes in favour of complete suffrage were ruined. From 1843 to 1845 there was a distinct improvement in trade and Chartism was losing its hold, although O'Connor tried to arouse new enthusiasm by launching his Land Scheme, a somewhat incoherent plan for purchasing land and restoring peasant proprietorship by distributing it by lot among the subscribers. This afforded him a new reason for opposing the Free Traders. The *Northern Star* advocated a land reform which would enable the country to be self-supporting—an ideal which, it was held, would necessitate a guaranteed price for corn. Through his paper O'Connor challenged any Free Trader to a public debate in which he was prepared to maintain that the repeal of the Corn Laws would not benefit the working classes. Cobden himself accepted the challenge, and, accompanied by Bright, appeared before six thousand persons at Northampton on 5 August, 1844. For some reason O'Connor did not put up a serious fight. His failure was generally recognized, and some Chartists believed that he had come to a previous arrangement to give Cobden the better of the encounter.

The harvest of 1845 was the final argument in favour of repeal. When the corn was in the ear, the rain began which "rained away the Corn Laws." Sir Robert Peel had evidently been open to conviction from the beginning of the agitation. He had readjusted the sliding-scale in 1842 so as to secure that prices should range, if possible, between 54s. and 58s. a quarter. In view of the bad harvest he was now prepared to go further, but he could not carry his Cabinet with him. Accordingly he resigned, and Lord John Russell, who had declared himself in his famous Edinburgh letter to his constituents of the City of London in favour of total repeal, was asked to form a Government. When he failed to do so, Peel returned, Protectionist opposition was overruled, and on 25 June the Bill repealing the Corn Laws passed the House of Lords.

The repeal of the Corn Laws probably prevented a revival of the revolutionary movement. In 1848, "the year of revolutions" on the Continent, there was no serious outbreak in England. Chartism did indeed organize a great demonstration in favour of a new petition to Parliament. It was arranged that a great meeting should be held on 10 April on Kennington Common to convey the Petition to Westminster. The Government was so alarmed that it enrolled nearly 170,000 special constables, and entrusted the Duke of Wellington, now approaching eighty years of age, with the supreme charge of the military precautions. O'Connor on his arrival at Kennington was told by the chief commissioner of police that no procession would be allowed to cross the bridges of the Thames, and that he would be held responsible for any disturbances that occurred. He consented to everything, and took it upon himself to advise the crowd to disperse. From this fiasco Chartism never recovered. O'Connor's course was now almost run. In 1847 he had been returned to Parliament as member for Nottingham, and he continued to speak occasionally, mostly on Irish affairs, until 1852, when, after a scene in the House, he was pronounced to be insane. He died in 1855, his funeral evoking a great popular tribute.

CHAPTER VI

THE CONSOLIDATION OF INDUSTRY

CHARTISM was a reaction against the Factory system; Free Trade was a recognition of its establishment, and an adjustment of national policy to meet its requirements. The Chartists stressed the class antagonism between the manufacturers and the wage-earners. The fight over the Corn Laws revealed a sharp divergence of interest between the manufacturers and the landlords. The consequences of these two oppositions were far-reaching. They would naturally suggest a possible understanding between the Tories and the Chartists against the manufacturers. In their protests against factory conditions the Chartists certainly had the sympathy and, to some extent, the support of the Tory party. Two sections may be distinguished. There were the Tory humanitarians, whose parliamentary leader was Lord Ashley. They were quite disinterested in their campaign for factory legislation, and closely associated, as, for example, in the Ten Hours movement, with working-class organizations in the North. But there were other Tories who saw that the exposure of the conditions in factories provided a good retort to the Anti-Corn League's insistence on the poverty of agricultural labourers. A violent attack was made, for instance, on the mill-owners, on account of their treatment of their operatives, by a Tory spokesman in the House of Commons in February, 1842. It was so strongly resented in Manchester that John Bright succeeded in getting members of the Exchange to pass a unanimous protest against the speech. The difficulties in the way of a Chartist-Tory alliance, however, were insuperable. They differed fundamentally about the extension of the franchise. And while they could unite in denouncing the Reform Act and the Poor Law Amendment Act, they did so for entirely different reasons. They had no common solution of the industrial problem unless it was its elimination—that is, they could agree, in their speeches at any rate, to refuse to accept the new conditions. The Factory system, they could insist, was an unhealthy growth which ought to be cut out of the social organism. J. R. Stephens, definitely, and Feargus O'Connor, with less consistency, took this view. Tory squires had their prejudices against industry, and Benjamin Disraeli lent them sufficient imagination to give their prejudices the illusion of convictions. A Chartist-Whig understanding presented difficulties of another kind. The Whigs had been responsible for one extension of the franchise, and, although they professed themselves satisfied with the results, they had admitted the principle of reform. They had been more influenced by Radicalism than their opponents, and from 1841 they were out of office. Consequently, they might be supposed to be more inclined to sympathize with the political programme of the Chartists. On the social side the Whigs were more committed to industrial development. Their commercial traditions always qualified their agricultural interests. Apart from the two main parties, which were already suffering from disintegration, there were the members of the

Anti-Corn Law League, representative of the manufacturers and acting with a handful of Radicals for the total and immediate repeal of the Corn Laws. They were offering cheaper bread, more employment, and higher wages. But their proffered gifts were suspected. The class-conscious Chartists insisted that they were the real enemy. Their economic beliefs were derived from the *laissez-faire* school, against which the whole body of Chartist teaching was definitely directed. But, in spite of all this, the League made steady headway among the working classes. Divisions within the Chartist ranks, one disappointment after another, and the apparent hopelessness of their agitation, all told in favour of the Anti-Corn Law League. On the question of cheaper bread their interests happened to coincide.

To accept the cheaper loaf was to accept the Factory system; for the loaf was to be made of imported grain which was to be paid for by exported manufactured goods. In 1846 there was really no alternative. The industrial system had been strengthening its hold on the country for half a century. G. R. Porter illustrated the development of various industries by the statistical tables in his *Progress of the Nation*, the second edition of which was published in 1846. He was able to show remarkable increases in the output of commodities. This was in part due to the growth of population, but mainly to improvements in production. Machinery had been generally adopted and steam-power had been applied not only to the driving of it but also to inter-communication. Industrial progress is often rather misunderstood, because the date of an invention is taken as more or less equivalent to the beginning of its general use. This is hardly ever the case. An invention requires a congenial environment. It was comparatively easy to introduce the spinning-jenny because it could be worked by hand and demanded no departure from the existing organization in the textile trades. The water-frame necessitated new arrangements: the use of water-power, a greater outlay of capital, and the securing of a supply of labour. The spinning inventions, however, were adopted speedily, for there was an existing strong demand for yarn. So spinning passed from the domestic to the factory stage comparatively quickly and without much friction; for spinning did not involve great skill, and was low paid and unorganized under the old conditions. But weaving has quite another history. Edmund Cartwright invented the power-loom for weaving woollen cloth in 1787, and two years later he applied steam-power to it. For a variety of reasons it was not generally adopted. In fact, after the invention hand-loom workers enjoyed a period of remarkable prosperity. The power-loom was a complicated machine. Its application to the weaving of cotton presented certain technical difficulties. No doubt these and other obstacles could have been surmounted had it been worth while. The hand-loom worker survived because, with an ample supply of cheap yarn, such profits could be made on cloth of all kinds during the war period that there was little inducement for manufacturers to invest money in power-looms. During this period of good wages the hand-loom worker established a higher standard of comfort and improved his position relatively to other workers. He had a real interest in maintaining his craft and wielded a certain amount of influence. Consequently the transition in weaving was comparatively slow, but, particularly in the later stages, appallingly disastrous. The weavers, as they grew older, found their wages steadily falling until they were a fourth of what they had been. A committee of inquiry estimated that there were still 840,000 hand-loom weavers in 1834. This covered cotton, linen, wool, and silk. Of these the cotton weavers suffered the severest hardships, for they had to meet the most serious competition from machinery. In 1803 there were only 2400 power-looms in the country, and in 1820 only 12,150; but in 1835 there were 90,000 employed in the cotton industry alone, and a total in all the textiles of nearly 100,000. The hand-loom weaver still clung to his craft because he was unsuited for or had no opportunity of getting other employment. In the later 'thirties and early 'forties the textiles were feeling the necessity for a wider market. All the conditions of an increasing output were present except a growing foreign demand. This economic position explains, from the industrial side, the phenomena already noticed. It was natural that men whose wages were steadily falling should bitterly resent the provisions of the Poor Law Amendment Act which deprived them of any outdoor assistance from the rates. At Ashton-under-Lyne, where the suffering from this cause was most acute, J. R. Stephens began his campaign against the Act. It was natural, too, that in the ranks of the Chartists the most extreme opponents of the Factory system were old hand-loom weavers. Nor is it difficult to see why the cotton manufacturers in particular wished to expand exports by admitting foreign corn.

It was not until the 'forties, then, that spinning and weaving were finally brought into line. They had become so predominantly factory processes as to make domestic workers extremely rare and, unless in very exceptional circumstances, unable to compete with machine-made goods. The fact that we still speak of factory legislation when we mean a code which covers a much wider field than is normally understood by a factory, is a reminder that the textile industries first drew attention to the new industrial problems. The early notice attracted by textiles is in marked contrast with the comparative lack of interest in the coal industry. "But for our command of fuel," says Porter, "the inventions of Watt and Arkwright would have been of small account, our iron mines must long since have ceased to be worked, and nearly every important branch of manufacture which we now possess must have been rendered impracticable, or at best have been conducted upon a comparatively insignificant scale." He gives figures to show that the quantity of sea-borne coals rose from 4,365,000 tons in 1819 to 11,380,000 tons in 1849. This includes coal shipped abroad and from one port of the United Kingdom to another, but excludes the large quantities carried by canal or railway. He estimates that 8,000,000 tons were consumed at the end of this period in producing pig-iron alone. These figures are really an indication of the general progress of industry, for the whole structure rested on the coal supply. But its importance was hardly recognized. Coal was produced in increasing quantities by methods which were unknown to the general public and by communities which were isolated and regarded as virtually uncivilized. The Report of the Royal Commission, which was appointed in 1840, at the instance of Lord Ashley, to inquire into the conditions of boy and female labour in mines, excited something of that mingled novelty and horror with which a cultivated audience listens to the description of the barbarous customs of a recently discovered tribe of aborigines. It is generally true that the mining populations were isolated geographically and socially from other sections of the community;[1] but in each district the methods of work and the conditions differed. In the Midlands the mines were usually worked by sub-contractors, who were responsible for a certain output and themselves employed the colliers. The pits were mostly worked directly by the owners in Northumberland and Durham, South Wales and Monmouthshire, and also in Lancashire. In Leicestershire, Yorkshire, and North Wales it was usual for the miners to contract with the owners through their own appointed heads. The growing demand for coal necessitated the resort to deeper seams and resulted in an increase of accidents from falls and explosions. The former were to some extent met by improved propping; and the latter had attracted the attention of Sir Humphry Davy, who invented his safety lamp as a safeguard against them. Still the number of accidents remained appallingly high, for the equipment of the mines was very inadequate and the system of ventilation by means of shutters, opened and closed by young children, was in general use until 1842. The majority of the mining population, men, women, and children, were often employed underground. The Commission reported in 1842 that young children sometimes spent twelve hours in the pits; women were working, usually as drawers, that is, in hauling away the coal for the getters, in Yorkshire, Cheshire, Lancashire, and

[1] Scottish colliers in the Lothian coalfield were hereditary bondmen until 1799. Cockburn, in his *Memorials*, composed between 1821 and 1830, after referring to this, continues: "These facts enable us to understand the hereditary blackguardism, which formed the secondary nature of these fixed underground gipsies, and the mysterious horror with which they were regarded, and which, in a certain degree, attaches to all subterranean labourers."

South Wales, and in some instances they were actually hewers.

Some of the grievances of the colliers were due to their isolation. The proprietors had to provide houses for their workpeople when a new pit was sunk. They also supplied the necessary provisions for the community. Out of the latter arose the iniquitous truck system against which the colliers long protested in vain. They were obliged to accept a certain proportion of their wages in goods of a quality and at a price over which they had no real control. Although there were Acts prohibiting this practice, the local magistrates often refused to put them into operation against the employers, and strikes for the enforcement of the law were unsuccessful. It is estimated that the total mining population amounted to about three-quarters of a million in 1840. From about that date it began to attract public attention and also to develop a self-consciousness of its own. Its isolation, in fact, had advantages, for the colliers could easily unite to defend and promote their own interests. With the growing importance of coal they came to exercise a more pronounced influence in the ranks of organized labour.

The demand for coal created by the iron industry has already been noticed. It increased enormously during the 'thirties and 'forties. Porter says that there were, on good authority, 452 furnaces in blast in the United Kingdom in 1848, turning out a total of over 2,000,000 tons of iron. The increase of output was stimulated by the developments in machinery and in locomotion; it was also facilitated by improvements in production which effected considerable economies. Among these the substitution of hot for cold blast should be noticed. J. B. Neilson, the engineer of the Glasgow Gas Works, demonstrated in 1829 that this method, despite the ridicule poured on it at first, was the means of saving 2 tons 18 cwt. of coal per ton of cast-iron. It remained for Budd of Ystalyfera, in the Swansea Valley, to show that the blast could be heated by using the hot gases that escape from the top of the furnace. Then in 1833 it was discovered that raw coal could be used in smelting provided that the blast was sufficiently hot. The immediate result was the establishment of a great Scottish iron industry. Up to this point Scottish iron production had not kept pace with that of England and Wales, partly because blackband iron-stone, of which extensive deposits were discovered early in the century, is not easily smelted, and partly because Scottish coal does not possess good coking qualities. These difficulties having been overcome, the output increased 700 per cent between 1835 and 1845. The most valuable deposits of iron-stone were in Lanarkshire and Ayrshire; and consequently the blast furnaces were concentrated in the district of Coatbridge, Airdrie, and Wishaw.

Economies in production reduced the amount of coal required per ton of cast-iron, but the cheapness of the iron so stimulated the demand for it that the total amount of coal used increased because a much greater quantity of iron was made. The introduction of steam locomotion very largely explains the phenomenal demand for iron in the 'thirties and 'forties. Porter computes that 615 Acts for constructing new railways and 496 for extending existing lines were passed between 1801 and 1849. The total sum which Parliament authorized the railway companies to raise between 1826 and 1849 he gives as £348,000,000. At the beginning of 1850 the aggregate length of completed railways in the British Isles was 5996 miles, of which 4656 were in England and Wales, 846 in Scotland, and 494 in Ireland. The expenditure on construction and equipment amounted to over £30,000 per mile. These figures were worth recording as some index of the revolution in transport wrought by the perfecting of the steam locomotive. They represent a capital charge as yet unparalleled in industrial development and a demand for coal and iron which made the adoption of all the new processes necessary and profitable.

The railway is much older than the locomotive. Railways, that is, prepared tracks made first of timber and later of cast-iron, were commonly used in connexion with collieries and canals; for loaded wagons could be more easily moved over such surfaces than hauled along the ordinary roads. The wagons were fitted with the usual wheels and retained on the rail by means of a flanged plate fitted to it which allowed them a certain amount of play. To William Jessop is due the idea of putting the flange on the inside surface of the wheel, thereby making a definite gauge necessary and speed possible. Wrought-iron rails, which would bear much greater strain, were not generally adopted until after 1820; the steel rail belongs to the second half of the century. The first steam-engines employed in connexion with railways were stationary, and used for winding wagons up a gradient or regulating the speed of their descent by means of a rope. Their heavy beams and condensing apparatus seemed to James Watt to preclude the possibility that the steam-engine would ever become a locomotive. Important experiments, however, were made in the early years of the century by Richard Trevithick (1771–1833) and John Blenkinsop (1783–1831), but it remained for George Stephenson (1781–1848) to show that steam locomotion was practicable. His first engine,

"My Lord," hauled thirty tons up a moderate gradient at four miles an hour in July, 1814. He retained Blenkinsop's principle of securing a regular motion by means of two cylinders working independently but assisting each other. The coupled engine in which two cylinders were attached to one pair of wheels was not introduced until 1826. Meanwhile, Stephenson had made some important improvements on his first model. He successfully employed the steam blast in 1815; and his opportunity to apply all his ideas came when he was appointed engineer of the projected Stockton and Darlington Railway. It was opened on 27 September, 1825—an important date in the history of railways—Stephenson's engine (which may still be seen at Darlington station) covering the distance at a speed of between twelve and sixteen miles an hour. Four years later he won the prize offered for the best engine by the promoters of the Liverpool and Manchester Railway. This locomotive, the "Rocket," was the direct forerunner of the modern engine; it was coupled, it had a powerful steam blast, and also the multitubular boiler which was designed to increase the heating surface. The formal opening of this railway on 15 September, 1830, was attended by a fatal accident. Huskisson (1770–1830), who represented Liverpool in Parliament, was travelling in one of the carriages, and at a halt for the engines to take water he and others got out. Noticing the Duke of Wellington in another carriage he went to speak to him, and before he could resume his place he was struck down by one of the engines and succumbed to his injuries a few hours later.[1]

[1] This accident naturally attracted much attention and confirmed the gloomy prophesies about the dangers of the new invention. Perhaps the attitude of the coachman in *Felix Holt* will be recalled. "His view of life had originally been genial, and such as became a man who was well warmed within and

The success of the locomotive marks the end of the canal era. The proposed railway from Liverpool to Manchester had been a direct challenge to that interest, which represented an invested capital of about £14,000,000, and it used all its influence to prevent the adoption of the new means of transport. Its opposition was supported by popular prejudice against what was considered to be a menace to public safety. An unfortunate result of this attitude was that the Government maintained a *laissez-faire* position, and consequently the landlords were allowed to charge excessive prices for land, and the railways were burdened from the outset by such heavy expenditure that they were unable to offer the facilities to the public which would otherwise have been possible. Companies also competed with one another for parliamentary sanction, all of them spending large sums of money, and there was no guarantee in the end that the scheme approved would best serve public utility. A Select Committee of the House of Commons, of which Gladstone (as President of the Board of Trade) was the chairman, expressed the opinion in 1844 that railway schemes should be regarded not merely as local improvements but in relation to national considerations of inter-communication. A special department of the Board of Trade, under the direction of Lord Dalhousie, was established for this purpose, but the speculative spirit became so strong that this restraint was set aside in 1845. The "railway mania" of 1845–6 resulted in the promotion of 248 Bills; shares mounted up to extravagant prices, and schemes were sanctioned

without, and held a position of easy, undisturbed authority, but the recent initiation of Railways had embittered him: he now, as in a perpetual vision, saw the ruined country strewn with scattered limbs, and regarded Mr. Huskisson's death as a proof of God's anger against Stephenson."

which could make no returns for years. A disastrous collapse followed, and in 1850 it was necessary to pass a Bill " to facilitate the abandonment of railways and the dissolution of railway companies," under the provisions of which several of the projects were dropped.

It had now become the accepted principle that the State should not interfere with individual initiative and free play ought to be given to competition. For years the Tariff system, which had become incredibly complex during the war period, had been suffering a modification in favour of the development of industry. The concentration of attention on the struggle for the repeal of the Corn Laws has tended to take it out of its proper setting. It was only the most striking incident in a movement which destroyed the whole Protective system. The withdrawal of the income-tax at the close of the war so embarrassed the Exchequer that for some years no comprehensive reform of indirect taxation was possible. A beginning was made in the 'twenties. The budget of 1824 has been called the first Free Trade Budget; the import duties on raw silk and wool were reduced and the prohibition on the importation of foreign-made silks was removed. Huskisson, who was then at the Board of Trade, was responsible for the reform of the tariff. He held that the removal of heavy duties would be followed by an expansion of trade. This belief was fully justified. The process of simplification, however, was hampered by the failure to find an adequate alternative source of income which would tide over a period of more drastic reconstruction. From 1838 to 1841 there were heavy annual deficits, and the Whigs revealed no financial capacity in dealing with the problem. The accession to power of Sir Robert Peel opened up new possibilities. In

1842 he effected a thorough revision of the tariff, but, to safeguard himself against a possible deficit as the immediate result of the extensive remission of duties, he revived the income-tax for four years. Formerly the income-tax had been regarded as essentially a war tax, but its use as a temporary measure in time of peace really meant that it was to become a permanent part of the annual income of the State, despite the fair promises of successive Chancellors of the Exchequer who held out the prospect of its withdrawal to their critics. With an estimated income of three and a half millions from this source, Peel was able to review the whole tariff, which still included some 1200 articles. His method of procedure shows the weight given to the needs of industry; he proposed to make reductions in 750 articles; raw materials if retained in the tariff were to pay a low or nominal import duty, partially manufactured goods were to be admitted at a considerably reduced rate, and manufactured articles were not to be charged more than 20 per cent *ad valorem*. So successful did these reforms prove that Peel asked the House of Commons to continue the income-tax for another three years, to enable him to undertake a second revision. In the budget of 1845 he provided for the removal of some 430 articles, chiefly the raw materials of manufactures. The following year witnessed the repeal of the Corn Laws. Gladstone's budgets of 1853 and 1860 completed the transition from Protection to Free Trade. There can be no question that the policy pursued, at long intervals, for nearly forty years suited the needs of the country. From 1836 to 1842 the distress was in no small measure due to the survival of a fiscal system which was a drag on the development of manufactures.

CHAPTER VII

EQUILIBRIUM

THE generation which had learnt its Radicalism from Cobbett and its Socialism from Owen had experienced little but disappointment in its efforts to realize the one or the other. The hope that society would be reconstructed by the immediate acceptance of some complete programme of political or social reform was therefore abandoned. More definite and restricted schemes were adopted as a possible means of working towards ends which were now recognized to be remote. Among these education must be given the first place. When the National Petition of 1842 was discussed by the House of Commons, Macaulay declared that it would be madness to enfranchise the masses until they were educated. His fellow-members entirely agreed with this view, though neither he nor they drew the conclusion that a national system of education was an urgent necessity. It must be remembered, however, that education had its champions among the working class all through the period of distress. They could not fail to imbibe from Robert Owen some of that enthusiasm for education which was behind all his other plans. Francis Place, from his own experience and his association with James Mill, set the highest value on it, and was engaged as early as

1814 in a project for a complete system of primary and secondary education in London. Later he was active in collecting money for the foundation of a London Mechanics' Institute for the instruction of adults. In 1824 the first series of lectures was given in the institution, which came to be known by the name of its founder, Dr. Birkbeck. Among the enrolled students were 1300 artisans. The movement spread throughout the country, and by 1850 there were 610 Mechanics' Institutes in England and 12 in Wales; but before that date the Institutes had mostly lost their hold on working men and had entered upon a period of decline. Adult education, in the absence of any systematic education in childhood, obviously presented peculiar difficulties. The Institutes began by paying too much attention to lectures on miscellaneous subjects, usually of a scientific nature. General elementary knowledge of what was conceived to be of a useful kind did not make a sufficiently strong appeal to prove a firm basis for an educational movement. F. D. Maurice (1805–72) and the Christian Socialists recognized the weak point in the Institutes when they proposed to establish Working Men's Colleges which would supply a liberal culture and foster democratic comradeship.

There were strong educational impulses in the advanced working-class movements. The London Working Men's Association put forward national education as an item in their programme, and their own activities, as originally conceived, were largely educational. Lovett spent much of his time during his imprisonment elaborating a national scheme: he demanded infant, preparatory, and high schools, the buildings to be used in the evenings for public lectures, readings, discussions, music, and dancing. To each school was to be attached playgrounds, gardens, baths, a museum, and a laboratory. He also wanted normal schools, agricultural schools, and travelling libraries. The whole was to be financed by voluntary contributions (for he was opposed to State control of education), to be purely secular, and democratically governed. He protested strongly against the view that the vote should be withheld until the people were educated, insisting that it was in itself an important means of education. On his release Lovett launched his National Association for Promoting the Political and Social Improvement of the People. He was joined by several of his old colleagues, and founded in the next year (1842) the hall in Holborn which was the one tangible outcome of his dreams. The Chartist movement, under O'Connor's inspiration, ran its course before Lovett's teaching was seriously heeded. After the failure of 1848 many old Chartists turned their attention towards education.

Others found an outlet for their energies in co-operation. Here again the inspiration came from Robert Owen. Ever since the New Lanark days he had taught the principles of co-operation. But it is characteristic of him that he did not confine himself to eliminating the middleman's profits and distributing the sum in dividends among the members. At New Lanark the profits were spent on education. Later he connected the distributive store with his conception of villages of co-operation. The members were to set aside their profits until they could purchase land on which they might settle as a self-sufficing community. Of these communities Queenwood in Hampshire was the most ambitious, and it ended in financial disaster in 1845. In the previous year, however, twenty-eight Rochdale artisans had founded a store which is recognized as the real beginning of modern distributive co-operation. The "Rochdale Pioneers" started with a capital of £28 representing the pound which each had saved towards the venture. They insisted on good quality, full weight, and no credit. The management was in the hands of the members and the profits were distributed in proportion to the purchases. By 1850 the membership had reached 600, there was a turn-over of £13,179, and profits amounted to £880. A quarter of a century later the membership was 8415, the turn-over £305,657, and the profits £48,212. The success at Rochdale gave a great impetus to the movement. In all the chief industrial areas the store became a prominent institution. At first it was intended to combine co-operative production with co-operative distribution. Mills were established at Rochdale the workers in which were to share the amount yielded by their labour after the shareholders had been paid a fixed sum. But the scheme proved a failure. The ideal of the self-governing workshop attracted considerable attention in 1848. It seemed to some a solution of the industrial problem; for, on the one hand, machinery could be fully employed, thereby increasing production, while, on the other hand, there would be no employers or any others drawing profits from the business. The wage system would therefore cease to exist. That this was not the dream of a few enthusiasts is shown by the reference made to it by John Stuart Mill in the second edition of his *Principles of Political Economy* (1852). "The form of association," he declares, "which, if mankind continue to improve, must be expected to predominate, is not that which can exist between a capitalist as chief and workpeople without a voice in the management, but the association of the labourers themselves on terms of equality, owning the capital with which they carry on their operations, and working under managers elected and removable by themselves." This anticipation of the course of industrial evolution has proved to be ill-founded. In spite of the most strenuous efforts to achieve the ideal there is little to record except a long series of failures. There is a marked contrast between the history of co-operation as applied to production and to retail distribution. The grocery store with its customers, whose weekly demand is fairly constant for certain commodities, has been the basis of an extensive business with a great variety of departments. In 1863 the local societies federated to form the Co-operative Wholesale Society, which began to manufacture goods for the branches. Its activities have come to cover an extensive field, but its methods do not differ in kind from those of private wholesale firms. The workpeople are employed in the usual way and receive wages : the highest claim that can be made is that the Society is a good employer.

The growth of the co-operative movement is almost entirely due to the voluntary effort of working people. The foundation, management, and extension of the societies represent an amount of energy and resource which cannot be easily computed, and, what is still more important, the prevalence of a certain point of view. There is nothing revolutionary about the movement : it is severely practical, and issues from a conception of self-help which is conservative enough. The same influence may be seen in the contemporary reconstructing of trade unionism and the development of friendly societies. The working class was beginning to yield to the dominant Individualist teaching. They were accepting the main ideas of the orthodox political economists. John Stuart Mill expounded these ideas in his *Principles of*

Political Economy, the first edition of which was published in 1848. It was regarded as summing up the economic discussions of the preceding generation and establishing beyond the possibility of dispute the main conclusions of the *laissez-faire* school. The *Principles* established and maintained a unique authority for the next quarter of a century. For this period, and in this sphere at any rate, Mill exercised the influence which his father, James Mill, intended him to wield when he carefully trained him to become the exponent of the Benthamite philosophy. The readers of the *Principles* did not realize the significance of the teaching of men like Hodgskin and O'Brien, who had supplied the Chartists with their economic dogmas. His treatment of Socialism is confined to a discussion of Owen's villages of co-operation and an account of the ideas of the French writers, Fourier and Saint-Simon. Consequently, the *Principles* effected a breach in the continuity of English Socialist speculation. It was not until the 'eighties that Socialist economics again began to exercise a wide influence through the popularization of the ideas of Karl Marx (1818–83), who, curiously enough, owed many of them to his forgotten English precursors. The orthodox political economy, therefore, owed much to Mill's sane and balanced exposition, and possibly still more was due to the apparent demonstration of its soundness which the prosperity following the repeal of the Corn Laws afforded.

The acceptance of the orthodox economics is well illustrated in the Trade Union movement of the 'fifties. After the failure of the revolutionary phase it had reverted to local trade clubs, and there was a strong suspicion of attempts at national organization. The unions as such took no definite part in the Chartist agitation. In fact, the trade unionists as a whole were opposed to any active participation in political propaganda, and they even condemned the resort to strikes in industrial disputes. The principles of supply and demand and, in particular, the conception of a wages fund, i.e. an amount set apart for the remuneration of labour which could not be increased by any effort on its part, had won general acceptance. It was held that wages were dependent on capital already accumulated, and they could only be augmented either by an addition to capital or by a reduction in the number of participants by a limitation of population. Hence the interest the trade unionists had in the insistence on a full apprenticeship and in the promotion of the emigration of workmen. They were in favour of the development of a better understanding between employers and employed and of the settlement of disputes by conciliation. Leadership was now entrusted to salaried officials whose point of view differed completely from that of the enthusiasts who dominated the movement in the early 'thirties. The most notable example of this new phase was the Amalgamated Society of Engineers (1851). Originally a number of local societies representing different sections of the engineering trade, this Society became a national amalgamation largely through the tact and energy of William Newton (1822–76). The principles on which it was founded affected the whole of organized labour in the 'fifties and 'sixties. It suggested a "New Model." The main characteristics were the limitation of membership to skilled artisans and the adoption of a firm financial basis. It attained the latter by combining the function of a trade organization with that of a friendly society. By this means considerable reserve funds were accumulated under centralized control. Friendly benefits were administered by the local branches, but the central executive, which was responsible for the general trade policy, had complete management of strike pay. Under the influence of the "New Model," unaggressive and remarkably responsive to the ideas of Individualism and self-help, the great modern unions took form and prepared themselves for the tasks which they had to undertake in the next generation.

Individualism had never regarded factory legislation with favour, and, while it had not been able successfully to oppose State intervention, it had exerted itself to limit such interference as narrowly as possible. Although the principles of State Socialism may be said to be inherent in factory legislation, this fact was not recognized even by the champions of regulation. Considerations of humanity or of common sense made it necessary for the community to safeguard itself against the more obvious evils of competition. Individualist theory, however, still held the field, though such a candid writer as John Stuart Mill saw that it was essential to reconcile it with existing facts. In the *Principles* he admits that in certain circumstances the State is justified in interfering with apparent freedom of contract, though this does not invalidate the general rule that each individual is the best judge of his own interests and should enjoy freedom to pursue them. He attempts to bring all legitimate intervention under three heads: (1) Sometimes the individual is not a good judge of his own interests, e.g. in the matter of education. (2) Children and young persons are not judges of their own interests, for in their case it is too often true that "freedom of contract . . . is but another word for freedom of coercion." They need protection against being overworked. (3) "There are matters in which the interference of law is required, not to overrule the judgment of individuals respecting their own interests, but to give effect to that judgment"; e.g. if certain employers desire to shorten the hours of labour they may be unable to do so because some of their competitors in the industry refuse to adopt a shorter working day. Here obviously some are to be overruled, but it is not clear whether it is because they are in a minority or because they are in the wrong. When this was written, children, young persons, and women were protected in a specified number of industries; adult men were not. The question of prescribing regulations where men were concerned was definitely raised by the proposal that machinery should be fenced even where none of the protected classes were employed. To oppose this and other extensions of the Factory Acts the National Association of Factory Occupiers was formed in 1855. Their agitation was supported by Harriet Martineau, who denounced the existing Acts as "meddling legislation," and it was exposed by Charles Dickens, who nicknamed it the Association for Mangling of Operatives. The Association, however, was sufficiently powerful to carry the Act of 1856, which it promoted in order to make any extension of protection by the fencing of machinery where adult men were employed very difficult. Even the Association did not dare openly to profess any intention to interfere with the Acts which covered protected persons. And since they were retained their application to other than textile industries was inevitable. At first new legislation was extended to such allied employments as printing, bleaching, and dyeing; then to pottery and hardware. In 1864 the making of lucifer matches and percussion caps and cartridges was scheduled as dangerous to health and life. Such extensions involved some definition of a factory, a question which was temporarily solved by the Acts of 1867, which differentiated between a factory and a workshop. The inspection of workshops—that is, of places where any handicraft was carried on in which protected persons were employed—was entrusted to the local authorities. Experience proved that this arrangement was unsatisfactory, and the whole series of Factory Acts, now exhibiting many complications and even inconsistencies, was reviewed by a Royal Commission in 1876.

The dominant note of the 'fifties and 'sixties was one of complacency. It seemed as though the root problems of industry had been solved and a future of peace and prosperity was opening up before the country. This was the spirit of the Great International Exhibition which was housed in the Crystal Palace (1851). But the fair prospect of peace was soon overclouded. The foreign policy of Lord Palmerston was highly provocative abroad and more congenial to certain elements at home than the gospel of peace, retrenchment, and reform. One international crisis followed another. In 1854 war was declared against Russia for the ostensible purpose of maintaining the integrity of Turkey, and the subsequent campaign in Crimea, with its military exploits and gross mismanagement, engaged the public attention for two years. Then followed the expeditions in Persia and China and the outbreak of the Indian Mutiny. These distractions, however, did not adversely affect the growth of industry: nor did the wars in Europe culminating in the Franco-German War of 1870. In fact, they contributed to strengthen the confidence in Great Britain's position as the chief manufacturing country of the world. France, hitherto the only serious competitor, was crippled, and Germany had not yet consolidated her position. Across the Atlantic the United States were engaged in the Civil War, which, although it caused great distress in Lancashire by cutting off the cotton supply, also postponed the day of the full development of America's industrial resources.

Contemporaries were inclined to regard the situation as normal. They did not give sufficient weight to the preoccupation of the chief Powers with non-industrial matters. A survey of the growth of manufactures certainly seemed reassuring. It is a testimony to the conviction of the merits of Free Trade that Disraeli, who had so virulently opposed Peel in 1846, accepted its principles when he became Chancellor of the Exchequer. Perhaps the most important new development was the discovery by Sir Henry Bessemer of a process by which molten iron could be directly converted into steel. This meant a great economy in fuel and therefore the production of cheap steel. It opened the "steel age"; before the end of the 'sixties it was used in making machinery, in shipbuilding, and in railway construction. For a time the British output of steel exceeded that of all the rest of the world. In this period the Cleveland iron deposits were successfully opened up, largely owing to the proximity of the Durham coking coal and the advantages of water transport. Consequently there grew up a great industrial area on the north-east coast.

Great Britain's position in the world market is sufficiently indicated by the increase in the value of exports. They were worth 71 millions sterling in 1850, 135 millions in 1860, and 199 millions in 1870. This enormous increase in the export of manufactured goods did not as yet affect the prosperity of British agriculture. Prices were falling, but, on the whole, the farmers were able to introduce so many economies in production that they did not suffer from foreign competition. That there was room for improvement is shown by the detailed account written by James Caird of a tour he undertook in 1850–1. He demonstrates that, while protected by the Corn Laws, much land had been neglected, landlords were often ignorant of the principles of estate management, and the contrast between good and bad farmers was very marked. Farm buildings were defective and the housing of labourers was scandalous. The prosperity of agriculture continued until the middle of the 'seventies. when it entered upon a period of acute depression. Several causes contributed to the postponement of the effect of foreign competition. The Crimean War had temporarily cut off the supply from the Baltic (1854–6), and the American Civil War (1860–4) interfered with export from the United States. Cost of production abroad and the expenses of transport were still too high to make serious competition with improved cultivation at home possible. The results of research in agricultural chemistry were widely known and adopted. In 1840 Justus von Liebig published his important work on the relation between the composition of the soil and the principles of plant nutrition. John Bennett Lawes, who inherited the farm of Rothamstead, had already begun the practical experiments which he prosecuted with scientific accuracy during the next generation. He tried to discover the true principles of the rotation of crops, manuring, and animal feeding. By treating phosphates with sulphuric acid he made them more soluble, thus producing superphosphate, a fertilizer which was extensively used until natural phosphates and basic slag became available. In conjunction with J. H.

Gilbert a chemical factory was established at Deptford. The work of Lawes and Gilbert is intimately connected with the second great period of agricultural improvement. Rothamstead was made a permanent Agricultural Experiment Station with an endowment of £100,000 in 1872. The drainage of land was stimulated by the Government, which authorized loans for the purpose repayable by instalments. Mention should also be made of the Royal Agricultural Society of England, incorporated in 1840, which did much excellent work in bringing the latest ideas before the wealthier farmers. The whole period was marked by a succession of good harvests ; the only great disaster being the outbreak of rinderpest in 1865–6, which is supposed to have come from Russia by way of Hull. It caused losses of stock amounting to about £3,000,000. This was a serious blow to breeders and dairy farmers, who had been distinctly more prosperous than the corn producers in the previous decade because of the growing demand for meat and butter and milk in the industrial areas and the virtual non-existence as yet of a foreign supply.

It must not be supposed that the agitation for the extension of the franchise was dropped after 1848. Chartism lived on, though now much enfeebled, until 1858 ; but meanwhile the Reform question was taken up by John Bright. He had deferred to Cobden's opinion that the Corn Law issue should not be confused by raising wider questions. When the repeal had been attained he had an idea of forming a new league to promote parliamentary reform. Cobden, however, placed his confidence in the middle class, which he thought could wield its power by taking advantage of the existing means of qualification. Bright's difficulties with the two political parties were also discouraging. The Whigs were divided: Lord John Russell was willing in 1851 to introduce a Bill, but he was opposed in the Cabinet by Lord Palmerston. After the conclusion of the Crimean War, Bright re-opened the question. He advocated what was called "household franchise" with an additional "lodger" qualification in October, 1858, not that he would not have gone further; but, as he pointed out to Joseph Sturge, anything more drastic would have no chance of acceptance. In a series of great public meetings he elaborated his proposals and aroused considerable enthusiasm. Disraeli tried to meet the agitation by introducing a Bill which gave the vote to certain special categories such as doctors, clergy, and university graduates. It met with so hostile a reception and was so strongly denounced by Bright that the Government was defeated. The Whigs were still divided, and Lord John Russell, since he could not carry Palmerston with him, refused to take up parliamentary reform. On the death of Palmerston, however, Russell became Premier, and, as he was now a member of the House of Lords, Gladstone undertook the leadership of the Commons. In the previous year Gladstone had pronounced in favour of the enfranchisement of working men. Consequently, the way seemed open for the introduction of a Bill in accordance with Bright's outline. But the Reform Bill of 1866 was defeated by the action of Robert Lowe and the dissentient Whigs who followed him into the "Cave of Adullam." The resignation of the Government was the signal for the renewal of Bright's public campaign. He won more widespread support than he expected, for the artisans, who had taken comparatively little interest in Gladstone's Bill, were alarmed by the defeat of such moderate proposals. A great demonstration was refused admission into Hyde Park on 23 July, but, while some accepted the refusal and withdrew to Trafalgar Square, others pulled down the railings and did a good deal of damage. This incident, of little significance in itself, helped to convince the Tory Government that something would have to be done. So Derby and Disraeli resolved to " dish the Whigs." A Bill, which in general terms enfranchised householders in parliamentary boroughs, that is, the majority of the artisans, passed the Commons and, since it came from the Tories, was accepted by the Lords.

CHAPTER VIII

NEW PROBLEMS

IT is a curious coincidence that in the year when the franchise was extended to include artisans in the boroughs a serious crisis arose in the trade union world. The very basis of the "New Model" was threatened by the decision of the Queen's Bench in the case of *Hornby* v. *Close*. Relying on the understanding that its funds were protected by the fact that it was registered under the Friendly Society Acts, the Boilermakers' Society had taken action against a branch treasurer for withholding a sum of money. The magistrates decided that it was not a friendly society, and their opinion was upheld on appeal; the High Court declaring that, though not criminal since 1825, a trade union was an illegal association in that it was "in restraint of trade." Much of the initial success of the "New Model" was due to the combination of trade functions with friendly benefits: the decision of the Court of Queen's Bench deprived them of the stability and safeguards thus given to their finances. In the same year public opinion had been aroused against trade unionism by a recent recurrence of industrial strife. For this the men were hardly to blame. Employers, alarmed by the progress of the movement, were attempting to curb it by using the weapon of the "lock-out," and consequently provoked retaliation. There were cases in which workmen had resorted to intimidation against non-unionists, and from Sheffield came reports of outrages which were exaggerated into general charges of sabotage.

Trade unionism, however, was now strong enough to conduct its defence. It had been very effectively organized in the previous decade by the officials of the "New Model" unions. William Allan (1813–74), secretary of the Amalgamated Society of Engineers, whose interest centred in administration, was in close touch with Robert Applegarth (b. 1834), secretary of the Amalgamated Society of Carpenters, who believed that trade unionists ought to take their part in promoting political and educational reforms. This view was strongly supported by George Odger (1820–77), the chief figure among London working-class Radicals. Together with Daniel Guile (d. 1883) of the Ironfounders, and Edwin Coulson (d. 1893) of the London Order of Bricklayers, these three constituted an informal inner cabinet of trade unionism, which has been called the Junta. Accepting the economic teaching of their time, they exercised extreme caution in trade disputes, always endeavouring to promote peaceful settlements. Although in favour of political reform, they knew that the rank and file were adverse to any entanglement in politics. So they had been working carefully towards the education of their members, particularly between 1858 and 1867, by the formation of trade councils which would give expression to local trade union opinion in the chief industrial centres. Allan, Applegarth, and Odger were prominent members of the London Trades Council, a body which assisted in organizing the popular welcome to Garibaldi, arranged a meeting in support of the Northern

States in their fight against slavery, and openly declared itself in favour of the Reform Bill of 1866. Other trade councils, on the initiative of Glasgow, agitated for the amendment of the Master and Servant Acts, which operated most unjustly; for, while a master could only be sued for damages in case of breach of contract, a servant was liable to imprisonment without the option of a fine for the same offence. As a result of interviews with Members of Parliament an Act was introduced in 1867 which removed the more serious anomalies of the law. It was a significant success, and marked the resumption of legislation dealing with labour.

The outcry against trade unionism in 1867 called into play and tested the organization of the previous years. The Junta realized that it had a great opportunity to justify the "New Model" trade unionism. Public interest was awakened, and there was a clear issue. Consequently, it welcomed the appointment of a Royal Commission to examine the work of the unions and to report on the alleged outrages. The Junta formed the "Conference of Amalgamated Trades" to supervise the case for the unions. It could also rely on the advice of an able group of sympathizers, including Thomas Hughes, M.P. (1822–96),[1] Frederic Harrison (b. 1831), and Professor E. S. Beesly (1831–1915). No working man had yet sat on a Royal Commission, and the Government did not depart from precedent. But Thomas Hughes and Frederic Harrison were members of the Commission; and Applegarth was allowed to be present at its sitting, and in his evidence he was able to show that his union was

[1] Author of *Tom Brown's Schooldays*; chairman of the first Co-operative Congress, and an enthusiastic advocate of co-operative production; principal of the London Working Men's College, 1872–83.

opposed to strikes and developed its business as a friendly society. It neither employed coercion nor did it keep any of its transactions secret. The employers, however, made the mistake of attacking the whole movement without discrimination and arguing against the principle of collective bargaining. They failed to make good their charges in the case of the "New Model" unions. This failure and the revelation that the Sheffield outrages were due to the action of members of local grinders' trade clubs prepared the public for a report favourable to the unions. The Majority Report, although not acceptable by the trade unionists, was by no means hostile; the Minority Report, which was signed by Hughes, Harrison, and the Earl of Lichfield, became the programme of the Junta. It recommended that all special legislation relating to labour contracts should be repealed and the following principles recognized: (1) That no act should be illegal if committed by a workman unless illegal if committed by any other person, and (2) that no act committed by a combination of workmen should be criminal unless it would be criminal if committed by a single person. Frederic Harrison also showed that the effect of complete legalization—which was favoured by the Junta—might prove disastrous. In his opinion the distinction between the trade and friendly society aspects of a union ought to be maintained. The unions should be brought under the Friendly Society Acts for the protection of their funds against the possible dishonesty of officials, but they should not become corporate entities which could be sued in the Courts. Otherwise, they would certainly be subjected to innumerable actions in which individual members or others would seek damages against them.

With a programme which required legislation it

was inevitable that trade unionists should use the vote they had just acquired. So in the General Election of 1869 parliamentary candidates were generally approached on the question. The Liberals, who secured the majority, passed a measure which temporarily protected trade union funds, but they were disinclined to go further. After some delay the Home Secretary introduced a Bill which provided that a trade union should not be illegal on the ground that it was in restraint of trade, that it should be entitled to be registered as a friendly society, and that it could not be sued in a Court for damages. To these clauses, however, was added another which forbade any violence, threat, or molestation in the conduct of a trade dispute. This clause was drawn in such general terms that it virtually ruled out all forms of picketing. It meant that in practice the privileges which the Government proposed to grant in the rest of the Bill would be of little value. The only concession the Cabinet would make was to separate the clause objected to from the rest of the Bill and embody it in a Criminal Law Amendment Bill. The two Bills became law. From 1871, therefore, trade union policy was directed to the effort to get the Criminal Law Amendment Act amended or repealed. Gladstone definitely refused to reopen the question. In 1874 his Government was defeated. The trade unionists ran several candidates in the subsequent General Election; where they did not, they gave their support to those who promised to see that the Act was amended. Two of their candidates were successful—Alexander Macdonald at Stafford and Thomas Burt at Morpeth, both of them officials of the National Union of Miners. Disraeli's Ministry introduced two Bills in the following year to amend the criminal and civil law. For the Criminal Law

Amendment Act they substituted the Conspiracy and Protection of Property Act, which set definite limits to the application of the law of conspiracy in trade disputes, and recognized the legality of "peaceful picketing." Also the Employers and Workmen Act took the place of the Master and Servant Act of 1867, and made employer and workman equal parties to a civil contract.

The legislation, which has been briefly summarized, represents a considerable change in the attitude towards trade unionism since the Acts of 1824 and 1825. They had been conceived on the purely Individualist principle that workmen should be free to combine if they wished to do so, but such combination was not to deprive either employers or employed of their contractual freedom. From 1825 to 1875 trade union action had been seriously restricted by the application of the law of conspiracy to cases in which there was any interference with the liberty of non-unionists or employers. Individualism approved of these limitations, and was still strong enough to influence Gladstone's Ministry to balance the Criminal Law Amendment Act against the Trade Union Act of 1871. The Junta, however, was resolved to gain greater freedom, and the subsequent trade union agitation secured from Disraeli the Conspiracy and Protection of Property Act. This amounted to the recognition of another principle, which in contrast with Individualism may be called Collectivism. Individual freedom of contract gives place to collective bargaining. Combinations of workmen are allowed, within certain limits, to bring pressure to bear on employers or strikebreakers. In fact, a distinction is drawn between trade and other combinations; an agreement to do an act "in contemplation or furtherance of a trade dispute between employers and workmen" is a privileged form of combination enjoying a latitude not allowed to combinations for other purposes. Without any breach of the law a trade union might now interfere with what individuals considered to be their freedom of action. This could not be justified on strict *laissez-faire* principles. From the Collectivist point of view there is no such difficulty. It may be necessary to overrule what the individual considers to be his own interest for the sake of the whole. Nor does this necessarily involve any loss of freedom; the individual may gain a greater freedom than that which he is obliged to sacrifice. To take a relevant and much discussed example: Suppose a workman wishes to exercise his freedom by remaining outside a trade union, but his fellow-workers (by legitimate means) compel him to join. His individual predilection is overruled; but, it may be argued, that he has been forced to surrender this in favour of the fuller advantage he will enjoy in union with the rest.

The election of Alexander Macdonald (1821–81) and Thomas Burt (b. 1837),[1] of the National Union of Miners, to Parliament in 1874 as the first distinctively Labour members draws attention to the growth of trade unionism among the miners. The progress which had been made in the 'sixties was largely due to the energy of Macdonald himself. He was the son of a Lanarkshire miner, and entered the pit at the age of eight. As a young man he saved enough to go to Glasgow University, and by working during the vacations he was able to stay there long enough to qualify as a teacher. He taught for a few years, and then took up what he

[1] The Rt. Hon. Thomas Burt was "Father of the House of Commons" when he retired from public life at the end of 1918.

made his lifework: an agitation to better the conditions of the coal-miners' life. Elected president of the National Union of Miners in 1863, he held that position until his death. His schemes were comprehensive, including effective regulation of the conditions of labour, the reduction of hours, the complete abolition of truck, and the right of the men to appoint checkweighers. At the Leeds Miners' Conference in November, 1863, Macdonald persuaded the delegates to divide themselves into sections, each charged with examining and reporting on special questions. The result was the elaboration of a complete programme of reform. The Conference, it is interesting to note, was opened with prayer by the Rev. J. R. Stephens, whose services to the cause of factory legislation and Chartism were recognized by his appointment as its chaplain.

As in 1833–4, so again in 1872–3, the period of great trade union activity affected the unorganized farm labourers. The leadership was taken by Joseph Arch (1826–1919) of Barford, in Warwickshire. He was an agricultural labourer who had shown great ability in such special work as hedging and ditching, and had often come into conflict with parson and squire as an outspoken Methodist local preacher. The movement, which he initiated by a strike for sixteen shillings a week, spread with extraordinary rapidity over the Midland and Southern counties. The National Agricultural Labourers' Union was formed, and its membership ran up to nearly 100,000. But it provoked the most determined opposition on the part of the clergy, squires, and farmers. In spite of the assistance of other trade unionists, the movement failed to hold its own. The agricultural labourer was too isolated from his fellows and too exposed to the observation of his masters for strong organization to be possible. Arch himself continued the fight for years, entering the House of Commons as Member for North-West Norfolk in 1885. He was a man of strong character, which was somewhat marred by his egotism and self-will. In politics he was a Gladstonian Liberal with very marked Individualist leanings; he believed in self-help, was suspicious of State aid, and opposed to land nationalization. His acceptance of the prevailing economic teaching is demonstrated by the amount of money his union spent in assisting labourers to emigrate; a policy which is said to have weakened its resistance by depriving it of its best members. The proposal to extend the vote to agricultural labourers may be considered as a political outcome of the movement. In 1884 Gladstone introduced a Bill to confer the same voting qualifications in the counties as were enjoyed in the boroughs. It was rejected by the House of Lords on the ground that it did not provide for a redistribution of seats. This was remedied in the autumn session, and a Redistribution Bill accompanied the Franchise Bill to the Statute Book.

The failure of trade unionism among farm labourers must in part be ascribed to the effects of the period of acute depression on which agriculture now entered. After 1875 the full effect of foreign competition began to be felt, and it coincided with a succession of very bad harvests at home. The English farmer was involved in a double misfortune; prices were falling and he had little to sell. Chief among the factors in the increased foreign supply must be placed the great extension of corn production in the United States which followed the close of the Civil War. During that contest it had been discovered that by adopting agricultural machinery the output of the prairie lands could be enormously increased with considerable economy of labour. The wheat production of Indiana, for instance, rose from 15,000,000 bushels in 1859 to 20,000,000 in 1863, although one-tenth of the male population was in the army. Between 1860 and 1880 the area under wheat in the United States was trebled, thus making it the chief source of supply in the world's markets. And by the building of railways and the improvement of ocean transport wheat could be carried at a fraction of the former cost. Production had also been resumed on the continent of Europe, after the conclusion of the Franco-German War. The natural protection which English agriculture had more or less enjoyed since the repeal of the Corn Laws was consequently eliminated.[1] The continuous fall in price would have adversely affected agriculture even if the harvests had been good; but the succession of bad seasons precipitated the disaster. "The Black Year" of 1879 was the worst. As the result of prolonged wet weather and the lack of sunshine the crops did not properly ripen, and disease broke out among the stock. It is estimated that three million sheep died or were slaughtered in England and Wales because of the prevalence of rot among them. Foot-and-mouth disease also played havoc with the cattle. A Royal Commission was appointed in 1879 under the chairmanship of the Duke of Richmond. It conducted a very full inquiry, which showed that the landowners and occupiers had suffered particularly in the corn-producing

[1] For the ten years preceding the repeal of the Corn Laws the average price of wheat per quarter was 57s. 10d.; from 1847 to 1856 it was 55s. 2d. Prices were well maintained until the later 'seventies. From 1875 to 1884 the average was 45s.; from 1885 to 1894 it was 30s. 6d.

counties of South-East England. Between 1879 and 1882 there were reductions in rent amounting to a fall in the annual value of agricultural land of £5,700,000. It recommended (among other things) that the local burden of taxation on land, which had been recently increased by the new education and sanitary rates, should be lightened—a recognition in itself of the relative decline of agriculture. The area under wheat continued to contract, and the rate of the migration of labourers from the countryside was greatly accelerated.

The depression of the later 'seventies was by no means confined to agriculture. The prosperity of the years 1867 to 1874 was followed by a serious collapse, which in its extent and severity was then unparalleled. Contemporary observers offered a variety of reasons for the disaster. The main facts were that the trade boom had chiefly influenced the iron, steel, and coal industries, and these were immediately affected by the crisis; there was an unprecedented fall in the prices of staple commodities, and these phenomena were not confined to any particular country. No simple explanation can cover all the facts. There had been undue speculation in railway construction in the United States and in shipbuilding in Great Britain, with its consequent demand for iron and steel in particular. The Franco-German War had stimulated the demand for British manufactured goods. But the war was followed by a period of dislocation; each country had to face its losses, and neither was a good customer in the world's markets. Some would ascribe almost everything to the scarcity and consequent appreciation of gold. In 1873 both Germany and Holland adopted the gold basis for their currency. The United States decided to convert outstanding paper money into gold. It followed that there was a great demand for gold to meet these currency requirements. At the same time there was a decline in the world's annual production of gold. So the price of gold went up, or, in other words, the price of all commodities—which is measured by the gold standard—fell. It would be as foolish to deny that this was a cause as to assert that it was the sole cause. The prices of different commodities were affected in different degrees; some fell more than the average and some less, but all fell. It seemed as though cheapness, especially of American corn and British manufactures, was spreading general ruin. This cheapness was of no advantage to consumers, not because their needs were satisfied, but because they could not afford to buy. So the crisis is sometimes explained as being due to over-production. This view was very generally expressed at the time. Improvements in the machinery of production, it was held, had increased the supply of commodities at a greater rate than that of the increase of demand. Whatever the causes of the crisis may have been, its effects on industry were well marked. The wages of miners, which were regulated by the selling-price of coal, were lowered step by step. In South Wales a third reduction provoked a disastrous strike, and the men had in the end to submit to a greater reduction than was first proposed. There was such a fall in the price of iron and steel that works had to close down. In Sheffield, out of 51 limited liability companies only 16 had their shares above par in 1880. Attempts were made in the textile industries to meet the depression by working short time and promoting emigration. Demonstrations of unemployed became a common feature in London and the great industrial towns.

The acute depression in agriculture and industry

naturally caused some misgivings about the merits of Free Trade. Since the repeal of the Corn Laws its principles had been accepted by the two political parties; Disraeli himself completely abandoned the cause of Protection. Free Trade, indeed, seemed to be fully justified by the prosperity of the 'sixties, which confirmed the forecasts of its advocates. On the Continent the Free Trade idea had also made considerable progress. Cobden had in 1860 negotiated a commercial treaty with Napoleon III, by which France had considerably reduced her customs tariff as against Great Britain. The Treaty which gave force to these arrangements included a most favoured nation clause, i.e., if France in any subsequent commercial treaty gave a lower tariff to any other country, Great Britain was automatically to get the same terms. As a matter of fact, she negotiated commercial treaties with Belgium, the German *Zollverein*, Italy, Switzerland, etc., with the result that Great Britain between 1860 and 1880 gained increasing advantages in the French market. This whole network of treaties by lowering tariff duties was working in the direction of Free Trade all round. In Germany the same presumption in favour of Free Trade is apparent in Bismarck's declaration in 1869 that "our fiscal policy ought to set itself the ideal of tariff for revenue only, even if it cannot perhaps be attained in its entirety." The current belief among intellectuals was that the world was making in the direction of universal Free Trade.

The tendency towards economic internationalism did not survive the trade depression of the later 'seventies. Germany adopted a new protective tariff in 1879 and France revised her commercial treaties in 1881. There were corresponding reactions in Great Britain. It was pointed out that other countries had not followed the British example. One-sided Free Trade, it was argued, was disadvantageous. Consequently, the Government ought to take steps to open foreign markets by imposing an equivalent tariff on goods imported as had to be paid by our traders when they exported to another country. The end of this retaliation was represented to be genuine Free Trade, for the foreign country knew that when it removed the tariff Great Britain would do likewise. Adam Smith held that retaliation might be good policy when there was a probability that it would effect the repeal of high duties. His authority and the fact that there was a growing excess of imports over exports were appealed to against the practice of one-sided Free Trade. But when Lord Bateman in 1879 raised the question in the House of Lords and pleaded for reciprocity in international trade, Lord Beaconsfield [1] assured him that reciprocity was dead. There had never been any real prospect that retaliation would result in mutual Free Trade. A much more specious attack on Free Trade policy was that which is known as Fair Trade. Its advocates demanded that all countries should be on an equality as far as the artificial conditions of production were concerned; for instance, if a foreign country paid a bounty on the export of any commodity an equivalent duty was to be charged on its import. Similarly, other advantages, such as protective duties, freedom from legislative restrictions, or the enjoyment of light taxation, were to be taken into consideration and neutralized by a carefully constructed tariff. Then the natural differences between countries would alone remain, and it was proposed that in this sphere free competition should operate. The chief feature of Fair Trade

[1] Benjamin Disraeli was created Earl of Beaconsfield in 1876.

is this distinction between the artificial and the natural conditions of production. In practice the distinction is so difficult to draw that it becomes rather unreal. The attempt to secure protection against artificial conditions while granting the principle of Free Trade where conditions were natural shows how firmly the latter was entrenched in England. It had to be attacked along a line which seemed likely to effect a split in the camp. For Fair Trade was Protection cleverly camouflaged. It was definitely advocated from 1881 by the National Fair Trade League, but with little success until the defeat of Gladstone on the Home Rule question. Lord Salisbury had on several occasions spoken favourably of Fair Trade, and he now appointed a Royal Commission to inquire into the causes of trade depression. The Minority Report expressed the views of the Fair Traders. The majority, however, held that it was " hardly worth while to discuss a scheme which involves at once a total upset of our present Budget arrangements, a reversal of our trade policy, and a breach with our foreign customers." The hope that the Conservatives would adopt Fair Trade as part of their official programme was doomed to disappointment. They had come into power in alliance with the dissentient Liberals, who called themselves Liberal-Unionists. Their leader, Joseph Chamberlain, was a strict Free Trader, and would not compromise his principles on this issue in the slightest degree. Consequently Free Trade survived the reaction.

CHAPTER IX

SOCIAL WELFARE

WHILE the principle of *laissez-faire* enjoyed a remarkable ascendancy in the middle years of the nineteenth century it was never quite unchallenged. The body of doctrine elaborated by Bentham and his disciples had proved potent in removing long-standing abuses. But when it had destroyed the old regulations and restrictions which had outlived their usefulness, it began to reveal a certain sterility in the face of the new problems which then emerged. In particular, it offered no firm basis for the building up of a tolerable industrial system. The depression of the years 1876 to 1882 brought home this fact to many who still clung to the formula of non-intervention, and had been unwavering in their allegiance to the orthodox political economy. The way was therefore prepared for a revision of opinion.

It has already been noticed that the Tory humanitarians who fought for factory legislation were necessarily contributing to the development of an opposing theory; although they hardly themselves recognized whither their principles would lead, for the Factory Acts were at first purely empirical efforts to remedy specific evils. A more definite indictment of *laissez-faire* is to be found in a succession of writers of the first rank. Robert Southey (1774–1843) has been called "the prophetic precursor of modern collectivism,"[1] for he powerfully supported the factory reformers in the 'thirties and incurred the censure of Macaulay for seeming to hold that "no man can do anything so well for himself as his rulers, be they who they may, can do it for him, and that a government approaches nearer and nearer to perfection, in proportion as it interferes more and more with the habits and notions of individuals." In *Chartism* Thomas Carlyle (1795–1881) declared a truceless war against *laissez-faire* as "a principle which this present writer, for one, will by no manner of means believe in, but pronounce at all fit times to be false, heretical, and damnable if ever aught was." Charles Dickens (1812–70) held the current political economy up to ridicule in *Hard Times* (1854). "It was a fundamental principle of the Gradgrind philosophy," he writes, "that everything was to be paid for. Nobody was ever on any account to give anything or render anybody help without purchase. Gratitude was to be abolished, and the virtues springing from it were not to be. Every inch of the existence of mankind from birth to death was to be a bargain across the counter. And if we didn't get to heaven it was not a politico-economical place, and we had no business there." Dickens never troubled to acquire any close knowledge of political economy, but there was enough truth in his caricature of it to be damaging to its teaching. John Ruskin, however, was well acquainted with the writings of the classical political economists, and his attack on their doctrines was a piece of genuine criticism. Although at the time the outcry against the essays,

[1] Dicey, *Law and Opinion in England*, p. 224.

which were afterwards published as *Unto this Last* (1860), was sufficiently strong to secure their discontinuance in the *Cornhill*, no one would now deny that they have considerably influenced the teaching of political economy. "Government and Co-operation," Ruskin asserted, "are in all things the Laws of Life; Anarchy and Competition the Laws of Death."

Neither Carlyle nor Ruskin was technically a Socialist, but their assaults on the *laissez-faire* position served to make a breach for Socialism to enter. There is curiously little, if any, continuity between the Socialist movement, associated with the name of Robert Owen, and that which began to exercise an influence over working-class opinion in the 'eighties. For nearly two generations Radicalism had been generally accepted. The Socialist developments on the Continent were imperfectly understood in England. In the meanwhile the whole outlook was being changed by the work of Karl Marx (1818–83) and his friend Friedrich Engels (1820–95). They were quite familiar with English industrial conditions—Engels published his *Condition of the Working Class in England* in 1845, and Marx, who settled in London in 1849, studied the growth of capitalism as it exhibited itself in England. His service to Socialism is that he eradicated that Utopianism which was so characteristic of Robert Owen and his French contemporaries. They looked for a sudden transformation of society, which they were optimistic enough to believe would be effected without violence. Marx insisted upon the principle of social evolution, and gave it a definite content by postulating an economic interpretation of history. If the actions of men are the result of the interplay of economic forces, an analysis of those forces, which are materialistic and measurable, should provide the key to human history. It would not only explain the past but reveal the future. Obviously a millennium or a New Moral World, as Owen called it, could not suddenly dawn. Evolution is a continuous process, and, if the forces in operation are known, it can offer no surprises. What, then, are the forces which are moulding society? According to Marx they are economic. At the very root of his economic analysis is the conception of "surplus value," an idea which he borrowed from his English precursors who had taught the right of labour to the whole product. The fact that others had contrived to appropriate a considerable share of the product explained the genesis of capitalism, or, in other words, capitalism was based on the appropriation and accumulation of surplus value. Consequently two classes developed in society, the bourgeoisie, which appropriated the surplus value, and the proletariat, which actually created it. With the command of constantly improving machinery of production the former tend to overstock the market and so provoke crises. The culmination will come when the proletariat are reduced to mere subsistence while the bourgeoisie, owing to the concentration of capital in the hands of comparatively few great concerns, are no longer able to control the industrial machine. Then capitalism will collapse, for the forces which created and developed it will be spent.

If the automatic working out of natural forces is to bring about the fall of capitalism there would seem to be no necessity for human action. But Marx was not a fatalist. In capitalist society there was an inevitable class struggle, but, when its true nature was fully exposed, the two parties conducted it with a self-consciousness which may appear incompatible with pure materialism. The bourgeoisie, on their part, could take steps to postpone the breakdown of capitalism, while the proletariat could hasten it. Marx, then, was not merely a theoretician; he was also a politician. He gave Socialism a systematic creed and also inspired the formation of Socialist parties in most European countries. He bequeathed them a difficulty which has been a cause of great dissension within their ranks. Should Socialists acquiesce in those social reforms which are tending to put off the day when capitalism will be overthrown? The Revolutionaries, claiming to be loyal to his teaching, denounce all palliatives. The Reformists accept any amelioration which is in accord with their general programme. In England the followers of Marx have never succeeded in forming a political party. The Social Democratic Federation, founded by H. M. Hyndman (b. 1842) in 1881, was a strictly Marxist body and its activities in the 'eighties contributed very considerably to the spread of Socialist opinions among the working class. But for one reason and another it failed to retain several of its most prominent members. In 1884 William Morris (1834–96) left the Federation and assisted in creating the Socialist League. Morris may be said to have retained in his teaching a good deal of that Utopianism from which Marx tried to purge modern Socialism. He was also opposed to any participation in politics, largely on the ground that it would necessarily lead to compromises which would tend to postpone the revolution. For Morris was convinced that there would be a revolution and that it would be sudden and complete. He was opposed to all such palliatives as could be obtained by political or even trade union action. The Socialist League also gave expression to the views on artistic craftsmanship which are intimately interwoven with his Socialism. Meanwhile, a third Socialist society had come into being with a policy which is partly indicated by its adoption of the name of Fabian. Its founders had never come under the personal influence of Marx, and apparently in the year of its foundation (1884) not one of them was intimately acquainted with his writings. In fact, it has been claimed that the first achievement of Fabianism was to break the spell of Marxism in England. It did not accept the doctrine of surplus value, nor did it stress the class war. The Fabians had no hard-and-fast system of economics ; as Collectivists they pointed out that under the existing arrangements individuals enjoyed the exclusive possession of wealth which was created by the community. They proposed that all such " unearned " income should be transferred to the State to be used for the promotion of the social policy which an enlightened democratic State would recognize as essential. This has been comprehended by Sidney Webb (b. 1859) in the conception of a National Minimum which should be secured for all citizens, namely, a minimum of labour, leisure, education, and sanitation. These were to be attained by permeation, that is, by bringing to bear whatever pressure or persuasion the Society might command on the existing political parties to induce them to move towards the realization of its aims. It was an intellectual circle with no faith in the policy of enrolling a great number of professed adherents. The influence it has wielded has been due to the investigations and teaching of a comparatively small number of workers. In this respect the Fabian group resembles the Benthamites, and it has been conjectured that the historian of the future will probably emphasize

Fabianism in much the same way as the historians of to-day emphasizes Benthamism.[1]

Of more immediate effect on public opinion was the publication of Henry George's *Progress and Poverty*. All competent observers agree that this book, tens of thousands of which were sold in cheap editions during the early 'eighties, stimulated the keenest discussion, particularly among working men.[2] Towards the close of 1881 Henry George (1839–97) himself had arrived in England to undertake a special lecture campaign. This was attended with remarkable success, and the English Land Restoration League was formed to recover the land for the people by George's methods. *Progress and Poverty* was first published in 1879 in San Francisco: it is a lucid exposition of a thesis which was by no means new, but it caught the public attention, partly because of its confident tone, and partly because it provided an answer to a question which was then uppermost in men's minds. The phenomenal increase in the production of wealth—so often held up to admiration as a proof of progress—was accompanied by the growth of poverty. Henry George offered a simple explanation of this paradox. The many were poor because the landlords exacted so much of the wealth of the community in rents. The remedy was also simple. By means of taxation falling on land values the wealth could be secured for the whole community and a more equitable distribution

[1] Ernest Barker, *Political Thought from Spencer to To-day*, p. 216.

[2] The interest taken in Henry George's theories was general: Ruskin met him when he landed in England; Arnold Toynbee's last task was two lectures on *Progress and Poverty* in London (1883); the Fabian Society discussed his teaching; A. J. Balfour read a paper on the subject to the Industrial Remuneration Conference (1885); and Herbert Spencer differed from him on land nationalization.

effected. Private property in land was, according to Henry George, in a different category from all other forms of private property; consequently, the Socialists, who made no such distinction, did not agree with him. The remarkable fact is that he had so little to say about specific industrial problems, and yet his message appealed strongly to working-class audiences in the towns. The land system, it must be remembered, was a grievance of long standing in England, and no doubt the spectacle of the recent hostility of landlords and tenant-farmers towards agricultural trade unionism had embittered feelings among the artisans. Joseph Chamberlain recognized this by giving the abuses of landlordism a prominent position in his Radical programme. It is also worth noticing that Henry George, while not strictly a Socialist, did more than any other propagandist in the early 'eighties to turn men's attention in that direction.

The general realization of the fact that there was a "social question" had a more profound effect on the formation of public opinion than the theories of any person or group. Inquiries, official and non-official, revealed the terrible housing conditions in the larger towns and the existence of "sweating" industries. There emerged a social conscience which felt that the evils were part of a system and not necessarily the fault of any individual, and consequently some social remedy would have to be found. The new spirit is illustrated in the establishment of settlements in the slums of London and other large towns under the impulse of members of the universities and religious bodies. In 1885 was founded Toynbee Hall, Whitechapel, as a memorial to Arnold Toynbee, and it became the scene of the life-work of Canon Samuel Barnett (1844–1913). Other settlements followed; some unsectarian, like Toynbee Hall, and some definitely associated with religious denominations. The evangelical passion to explore and rescue " Darkest England " inspired the formation of General Booth's Salvation Army (1878) with all its subsequent equipment of shelters, workshops, and emigration agencies. A more scientific survey of the extent and nature of the problem was provided by the investigations of Charles Booth and his collaborators in *Life and Labour of the People in London,* which served as a model for such local inquiries. His census showed that 32 per cent of the inhabitants of London were below the line which divided those who enjoyed the possibilities of a decent life from those who did not.

After its successes in the 'seventies trade unionism had fallen back into the old grooves. The leaders avoided strikes and husbanded the resources of their unions to meet the claims of sick and other benefits. They were still under the influence of the orthodox political economy, although Mill himself had abandoned the wages-fund theory which had so long discouraged an aggressive policy.[1] As far as they took any interest in politics they supported Gladstonian Liberalism. This attitude, however, could not survive the ferment of the 'eighties. The younger men denounced the Individualism of the leaders and openly advocated Collectivist ideals. Prominent among these rebels were two members of the Amalgamated Society of Engineers, Tom Mann (b. 1856) and John Burns (b. 1859), who insisted that their Union was becoming ineffective. John Burns asserted that the " reckless assumption of the duties and responsibilities that only the State or whole community

[1] Mill discarded the theory in his review of W. T. Thornton's book *On Labour* in 1869.

can discharge, in the nature of sick and superannuation benefits, at the instance of the middle class, is crushing out the larger unions by taxing their members to an unbearable extent. . . . The result of this is that all of them have ceased to be unions for maintaining the rights of labour, and have degenerated into mere middle and upper class rate-reducing institutions." Both Burns and Mann were members of the Social Democratic Federation; Burns speaking for it at the Industrial Remuneration Conference (1885), when he very significantly drew attention to the Socialist principles at the back of the activities of the great municipalities.

The "New Unionism" made great headway in the later 'eighties. Its leaders appealed especially to unskilled labourers, who were practically unorganized; for the older unions were exclusive, partly owing to the comparatively high contribution they had to charge to meet their obligations in friendly benefits, and partly because they insisted on a full period of apprenticeship as a condition of membership. The new unions did not propose to hamper their trade policy by performing the functions of friendly societies; the only charges on their funds were to be victimization and strike pay. Their trade policy was frankly aggressive and their ultimate aims distinctly Socialistic. To the older men the movement seemed dangerously extreme, and their resistance led to a stiff contest within the trade union ranks. But events favoured the progressives. They were given a series of advertisements which familiarized the whole country with the developments in London. On 8 February, 1886, a meeting for unemployed was held in Trafalgar Square. Members of the Social Democratic Federation insisted on addressing it. The temper of the crowd was aroused, and it broke up into parties, which marched through Pall Mall, St. James's Street, and Piccadilly, breaking the windows of the clubs and doing what other damage they could. The alarm occasioned by this outbreak was renewed by the events of Sunday, 13 November, 1887, when an attempt was made by a great body of Radical and Socialist demonstrators to hold a meeting in Trafalgar Square in spite of the prohibition of the Chief Commissioner of Police. The police were ordered to break up the processions before they arrived at the Square, but both infantry and cavalry had to be summoned to their aid. The demonstrators fought with great determination, particularly at the corner of the Strand. Two leaders —John Burns and Cunninghame Graham—broke through the police cordon, and were condemned to six weeks' imprisonment for their share in the affray.

The demonstrations of the unemployed were followed by a series of strikes which revealed the spirit of the "New Unionism." In some ways the most remarkable was that of the London match-girls in 1888, for they had no reserve funds and no organization, and yet their action was so strongly supported by public opinion that they succeeded in winning concessions from their employers. Mrs. Annie Besant had both inspired the revolt of the girls against the conditions of their employment and had taken care to bring the facts before the public. This kind of appeal, it was discovered, met with a widespread response; a fact which is an indication of the growth of the social conscience. In the next year the Gas Workers and General Labourers' Union was founded, and, having enrolled some thousands of members, it demanded a reduction of hours from twelve to eight. This claim was conceded without a contest. Encouraged by this unexpected success, Ben Tillett (b. 1859), who had failed to organize the dock labourers in 1886, returned to the task. It presented peculiar difficulties. The men attended daily at the dock gates, and those required were engaged for a certain number of hours by contractors to whom the dock companies entrusted a particular job. Normally the applicants greatly exceeded the demand, and consequently only a fraction of them would be employed and many of these for a few hours. An individual labourer who secured work for some portion of three or four days a week could count himself fortunate. Such a floating mass of casual labour offered hardly any opportunity for organization; the reserve which always existed was a menace to those who had any design of withholding their labour as a protest against the conditions. On 13 August, 1889, however, a dispute arose on the South-West India Dock which quite unexpectedly precipitated a great strike. The men demanded the abolition of the contract system, a minimum engagement of four hours, a rise from fivepence to sixpence an hour, and extra pay for overtime. In a few days the Port of London was at a standstill. Ben Tillett was joined by John Burns and Tom Mann. They organized their forces with remarkable skill, preventing the men from spoiling their case by violence of any kind, and defeating every attempt of the dock companies to break the strike by introducing blacklegs. The sympathy of the public was enlisted, and never forfeited during the five weeks' struggle. Contributions amounting to over £48,000, of which £30,000 was cabled from Australia, enabled the leaders to establish a complete system of strike pay. The attitude of the dock companies was generally condemned, and they had to acquiesce in the conduct of negotiations by a few prominent citizens, including Cardinal Manning, the Bishop of London, and Sydney Buxton, then Member of Parliament for Poplar. A settlement was arrived at on 15 September, the strikers practically securing all they had demanded.

The London Dock Strike was a victory for unskilled men with no traditions of organization behind them. It was also a vindication of the claims of "New Unionism." Out of it sprang an enthusiasm for trade unionism which, it is estimated, increased the total membership by about 200,000 within twelve months. Not only did unions of general workers enroll the unskilled in all the chief ports, but the older craft unions felt the influence of the new spirit. They relaxed their rules to admit new elements, with the inevitable result that their whole attitude was gradually modified. At the time there was considerable apprehension about the consequences of the trade union revival. To some it seemed ominous that disputes were not limited to demands for advances in wages, but often involved questions of the conditions of labour which were regarded as the business of the management. Others feared that the Socialists would turn the movement in a revolutionary direction. They confounded the statements of the Social Democratic Federation with the policy of the "New Unionism." There was no excuse for this identification after the withdrawal of John Burns and Tom Mann from the Federation in 1889. The alarmists overlooked two important facts. In the first place, the rank and file of trade unionism was by no means Socialist, and its representative body, the Trade Union Congress, was still dominated by the older leaders whose Individualism represented a lifelong conviction. The contest between the two parties was renewed in the annual

Congress for some years. It was not until 1899, for instance, that the Congress accepted the principle of direct labour representation in Parliament. In the second place, the leading exponents of the "New Unionism" believed in working through existing democratic institutions. They pointed out that the reforms, parliamentary and municipal, of the nineteenth century offered opportunities for realizing their aims by constitutional methods. John Burns perhaps will be chiefly remembered as a great municipal reformer with an unparalleled knowledge of and enthusiasm for London.[1] He was elected a member of the newly constituted London County Council in the spring of 1889. Everywhere the "New Unionists" were encouraged to play their part in local administration and to exploit to the full the possibilities of bettering conditions which the local representative bodies possessed.

The Municipal Corporations Act (1835) had not been applied to London. Apart from the cities of London and Westminster, which were governed by their respective corporations, the Metropolitan area consisted of separate parishes, each responsible for local administration. In the 'fifties the improvements effected in other towns by the representative bodies established under the provisions of the Act of 1835 led reformers to make a renewed attempt to bring the government under a single authority. The result was the Metropolitan Management Act

[1] Patrick Geddes has often pointed out London is not so much a city as a collection of cities; a trading port on the East, an imperial capital at Westminster, a financial centre in the "City," and innumerable "dormitory extensions." A proper civic consciousness is difficult to attain. "Think how free (the Londoner) has been from any feeling of pride of citizenship . . . until John Burns and his fellow-senators of the London County Council began to put some proper civic spirit into him." Geddes and Slater, *Ideas at War*, p. 231 and chap. xi. *passim.*

(1855), which created for the whole of London the Metropolitan Board of Works. The Board consisted of delegates from the vestries of the various parishes, and was entrusted with powers to improve streets and drainage and to provide parks and open spaces. Although the Board did some good work, it was not a satisfactory solution of the problem of self-government. London did not possess an authority which could follow the example of Manchester, Liverpool, Birmingham, and Glasgow. The County Councils Act of 1888 provided an opportunity for superseding the Metropolitan Board and forming the County of London with its representative Council charged with extensive duties over a wide area. Within the next decade the Council, which was profoundly influenced by the opinions of the Fabian group and the enthusiasm of the " New Unionists," effected important reforms which have left a permanent mark on London.

Meanwhile the boroughs, which were given or qualified for representative institutions under the Act of 1835, had made many interesting experiments. They found that, as a general governing authority for the whole locality, with the power to levy rates and responsibility for " the good rule and government of the borough," they had to undertake one scheme after another. Their first efforts were directed to the improvement of public health. In the early years of the nineteenth century the sanitary condition of the towns, particularly of the new industrial centres, were scandalous. Population was settling where factories were erected, and no kind of public control was exercised over speculative builders, and no provision was made for proper drainage or a water supply. The first visitation of the cholera in 1831 drew attention to the question. Edwin Chadwick (1800–90), who had been a private secretary to Jeremy Bentham and became secretary of the Poor Law Commission, opened a campaign against preventable disease. Lord John Russell was induced to order a general inquiry (1839), and Chadwick virtually directed the procedure especially to the examination of housing conditions, the water supply, the removal of refuse, and drainage. In 1842 he published his *Report on the Sanitary Condition of the Labouring Classes of Great Britain*. Parliament refused to take any steps to remedy the evils exposed by the inquiry, but in 1844 agreed to the appointment of a Royal Commission on the Health of Towns. The evidence confirmed Chadwick's main contentions, and the second visitation of the cholera (1847) moved it to establish a Board of Health to advise on matters of public health and to form local boards. The Central Board, of which Chadwick and Lord Ashley were members, suffered from a double weakness: the formation of local boards was optional unless the death-rate exceeded 23 per thousand; and the Board itself was temporary, its powers being granted for five years. The consequence was, that all vested interests opposed the efforts of the Board to effect reforms in the hope that Parliament would allow it to lapse at the end of the period. Cholera raged again in 1853 and 1854, and Chadwick's plea that pure water and good sewage were the best means of combating it slowly won general acceptance. The Board of Health came to an end in 1854, and no central authority exercised a definite supervision over local administration until the Public Health Act of 1875, which empowered the newly constituted Local Government Board to impose regulations on the local authorities.

The development of municipal government had qualified the local bodies to undertake these and other responsibilities. But there were misgivings about the extension of public enterprise. To the Individualists there were two main objections. They believed that private initiative would be more efficient in performing any task than a public body. Ultimately this belief was based on the supposed merits of competition. In most cases, however, competition was necessarily ruled out, for the supply of water, gas, or even of tramway services, will not be undertaken by a private firm unless it is guaranteed a monopoly. It was also feared that the provision of so many services by the community would undermine the sense of individual responsibility. As a matter of fact, the extension of the area of public action, while it has relieved the citizen of certain obligations, imposes new responsibilities of a higher kind, and provides services and amenities which he could not secure for himself by his own efforts. To the activities of the local authorities must be ascribed some of the main differences between the conditions under which the ordinary person lived at the beginning and the end of the nineteenth century. The population became largely town-dwelling, and consequently unable to secure its needs in separate self-sufficing households. Communities performed the functions required by the new conditions: they paved the streets, arranged for lighting and cleansing, supplied water, gas, and electric light to private houses, organized means of transport, established schools, libraries, museums, and art galleries, laid out parks and recreation-grounds, and gave special attention to child welfare. Some of the results can be read in the vital statistics—the fall in the death-rate and in the figures of infant mortality. Others are so familiar as to be often overlooked. All of them constitute an imposing plea for the solution of social problems by communal effort. The realization of this fact explains why the enthusiasms of the 'eighties found an outlet in municipal reform. To John Burns, for instance, the achievements of the progressive municipalities demonstrated the practicability of Socialism, and the existence of representative local institutions challenged all reformers to attempt to attain their purposes through them.

CHAPTER X

THE ORGANIZATION OF INDUSTRY

INDUSTRIAL development in the last quarter of the nineteenth century clearly revealed new forms of organization; for under the stress of competition at home and abroad capitalism necessarily suffered modification. But the nature and extent of the change were so little appreciated that it was generally assumed that the conditions of the earlier part of the century survived. Industry was thought of as still divided into a number of separate businesses, each competing with the rest, and directed by an individual capitalist who secured for himself the profits of successful enterprise. This free competition was supposed to guarantee to the consumers an ample supply of commodities of good quality at a fair price. Assumptions of this kind were indeed at the root of the accepted economic theory. Adam Smith was so convinced that individual initiative was essential to success that he did not anticipate that the joint-stock principle would be applied to the ordinary business. And Karl Marx himself based his law of the concentration of capital on the supposition that each business was managed by a single person. In his opinion businesses would become larger, and consequently the number of capitalists would decrease and the ranks of the proletarians would be strengthened.

He did not foresee that capitalism would entrench itself by bringing into existence a large class of persons who draw their income from investments in industrial ventures and are therefore interested in the maintenance of the system. Capitalism has never actually resulted in free competition. The ideal was most nearly realized in the middle years of the nineteenth century. But legalization of limited joint-stock companies in 1862 may be regarded as a new point of departure; and since the 'seventies the tendencies towards closer concentration and the elimination of competition have become increasingly apparent.

The growth of industry has not been marked by a corresponding increase in the number of units of production. Factories and works required such a great outlay on machinery that the total capital invested came to be a much more considerable sum than the annual wage bill. It was easier to extend existing businesses than to found new ones —that is, individual firms employed larger numbers of workpeople. This concentration naturally suggested further economies by bringing under a single control allied processes which were originally distinct; for instance, an iron and steel works might secure its own ore deposits, buy tramp steamers to carry it, acquire coal-mines for its fuel, and also develop industries to dispose of its by-products. The best examples of such unified control are to be found in Germany and the United States. But they are by no means unknown in Great Britain. International competition became so keen that the aggregation of industries which had been carried on separately was essential; the cheaper forms of wire products, for example, could not hold their own in the world's markets if they were subjected to disadvantages of the following nature: a steel billet might be sent from Middlesbrough to Warrington to be rolled into a wire rod and then dispatched to Birmingham to be drawn into fine wire. The aggregation of these processes would eliminate the waste in transport and make other economies possible. The consequent enlargement of a single works would probably be followed by further extensions of a similar kind. It would also reduce the number of firms in any particular industry, and thereby facilitate understandings between them which would rule out genuine competition. This monopolistic tendency is obvious in the American Trusts and the German Cartels. There are, however, many forms of the movement which cannot be so easily identified. In the Trust, different firms are under the control of a small centralized committee exercising such extensive powers that their separate individuality is practically lost. Germany affords in the Cartels examples of agreements between firms which cover amount of output and selling price but allow to the members more voice in the direction of general policy. In Great Britain amalgamations and agreements have secured the same main purposes, although Free Trade precludes the possibility of giving such assistance to combines as they enjoy elsewhere in the form of bounties, subsidies, and preferential tariffs.

The operation of the force of competition has therefore been defeated by general tendencies, which may be regarded as self-protective developments of capitalism itself. With the growing costliness of modern equipment this was inevitable; some means had to be found to remedy the considerable mortality among small competing firms which characterized the earlier phases of industrialism. When ventures are on a sufficiently large scale they take care to assure themselves of the conditions of success. Side by side with the growth of these inherent qualities of capitalism must be placed other considerations, which have from the outside restricted its development in certain directions. If it be true that industry cannot endure unlimited competition, it is still more obvious that society, as long as inequalities remain, cannot rest on pure freedom of contract. It has to protect itself against the complete working out of the implications of capitalism. This it has done partly by the action of the State and partly by recognizing the existence and activities of voluntary associations. The best examples of these two methods are factory legislation and trade unionism. In the former, the State interferes to prescribe certain common rules which are to be followed in the conduct of industry; in the latter, the wage-earners combine to safeguard their interests. Each movement had to contend against strong opposition for the greater part of the nineteenth century, and even the advocates of the one or the other did not realize the part they were playing in effecting the stability of the capitalist State. Their function becomes clearer if it be supposed that one of the methods had been adopted to the exclusion of the other. If society had defended itself against the possible anti-social consequences of industrialism solely by State action, the sphere of control would have been a great deal wider than it was in 1914. Bureaucratic Socialism would have been a reality. Had the provision that every one should work been added to the elaborate code drawn up to protect the individual from insecurity and want, what has been called the Servile State would have come into being. On the other hand, if it had been left to the wage-earners to provide a competent defence against possible exploitation, their organizations would have had to perform so many functions that the State would have become relatively unimportant. The logical consequence would be the establishment of Syndicalism. In actual practice, however, tendencies are always modified by the emergence of correctives before they arrive at a simple solution of complex problems.

In England the presumption in favour of political action, which is so marked throughout the nineteenth century, was strengthened by the successive extensions of the franchise. It was generally believed that conditions could be improved by the use of the means offered by representative institutions. The Socialists, particularly under the influence of the Fabian Society, paid special attention to the problems of local government and the social possibilities of municipal enterprise. They also had ambitions to secure representation in the House of Commons. Such Labour members as had already been returned—as, for instance, Thomas Burt, Joseph Arch, and William Abraham—attempted to work through the Liberals, and were mostly associated with that Party on general political questions. The Social Democratic Federation had run three of its members in the elections of 1885, but, with the exception of John Burns, who contested West Nottingham, the candidates won hardly any support. The Federation, however, did not pursue its efforts to gain political representation with any consistency, and the rigidity of its creed prevented it from making a sufficiently wide appeal to carry elections. The question of a Labour Party, which would act quite independently in the constituencies and the House of Commons, was taken up by J. Keir Hardie (d. 1915). His ideas found expression in the Independent Labour Party (1893), a definitely

Socialist body without the doctrinaire strictness of the Social Democratic Federation. It was to be a political organization through which Socialist opinions would carry what weight they could in Parliament. In the General Election of 1892 John Burns and Keir Hardie himself had been returned for Battersea and South-West Ham respectively.

To become really effective a political Labour Party needed the backing of the industrial organizations. The difficulty which the Socialists experienced in the 'nineties in their attempt to secure the co-operation of the trade unions was due to the hold which the traditional political parties still had in the constituencies. There was no opposition to political action on the ground that it was likely to prove less powerful than industrial or "direct" action. Both parties in the Trade Union Congress, where the question was discussed every year, believed in political action; the Socialists wished to exercise it uniformly by means of an independent Labour Party, while their opponents stood for the existing arrangement by which the unions brought political pressure to bear on the Government when a specific grievance needed a remedy. The contest ended in 1899, when the Trade Union Congress directed its Parliamentary Committee to summon a conference in conjunction with the Socialist societies[1] "to devise ways and means for securing an increased number of Labour members in the next Parliament." As a result of their deliberations the Labour Representation Committee was formed, charged with the duty of promoting Labour candidates for Parliament. The provision of this joint machinery might have had little immediate effect if the position of trade

[1] There were now three: The Social Democratic Federation, the Fabian Society, and the Independent Labour Party.

unionism had not been endangered by the Taff Vale Judgment (1901). An action had been brought against the Amalgamated Society of Railway Servants for damages on account of the alleged conduct of its members during a strike in South Wales. Relying on the understanding that the Society was not a corporate body—and no action for tort had ever been allowed against an unincorporated group—the answering plea was made that the Society itself could not be sued. Judgment was given, however, against the Society on the ground that the law had not intended to establish associations holding property and performing important functions without being responsible in damages for any wrongful act. The judgment was reversed by the Court of Appeal, but finally upheld in the House of Lords. Its effect was to withdraw the protection which it was supposed trade union funds enjoyed under the legislation of the 'seventies. They were practically reduced to impotence, for peaceful picketing might well be construed as illegal in any particular instance and the union in the interests of which it was adopted heavily fined. The Trade Union Congress recognized that strong political action was necessary to safeguard the movement against the depletion of its funds by a series of actions for damages. It was, therefore, resolved to demand legislation which would remove this danger. Consequently, the cause of independent parliamentary representation received a new impetus. In the General Election of 1906 the Labour Party won twenty-nine seats.

The new Parliament seemed to offer every opportunity for realizing the programme of social reform which the progressive elements had perforce to drop during the Boer War. Events had contributed to make organized labour inclined to accept the view that legislation would remove the chief social evils. The first demand the Labour Party put forward was that trade unions should be protected against the consequences of the Taff Vale Judgment. The Bill which the Government introduced for this purpose proved unacceptable, but under pressure it was withdrawn and the Labour Party proposals substituted for it. This success in the narrower field of trade union legislation was the most notable that Labour achieved in Parliament. By means of the Bill—which became the Trade Disputes Act (1906)—a trade union was given virtual immunity against civil actions, and its funds were adequately protected. But the wider schemes of the Labour Party, as, for instance, the Right to Work Bill, which was an attempt to meet the problem of unemployment by imposing statutory obligations on the local authorities, were not realized. It was reduced to supporting the Bills promoted by the Government or trying to obtain amendments which in its opinion would strengthen them. Its critics could assert that there was nothing distinctive about its policy. Old Age Pensions (1908), for example, had been under discussion for some years, and may be regarded as arising naturally out of the more generous treatment which the aged as a class had been receiving from the Poor Law Authorities. No section of the House of Commons was prepared to incur the opprobrium of strongly opposing the proposal, although some would have liked a contributory basis. The co-operation of trade unions was invited in the working of Labour Exchanges, which were set up in 1909 under the supervision of the Board of Trade; but this method of reducing the volume of unemployment by facilitating the mobility of labour was a commonsense reform which did not involve any new attitude towards the main problem. On the question of National Insurance (1911), covering sickness and unemployment (in certain trades), the Labour Party differed from the Government on several important points, particularly with respect to compulsory contributions, but they failed to satisfy a considerable section of their supporters by their handling of the matter.

A definite reaction against Parliamentarianism may be detected from 1910 to 1914. Much of this is to be ascribed to the disappointment of the hopes of 1906; the actual results of direct Labour representation seemed to be meagre, and Parliament was involved in one difficulty after another as it attempted to deal with education, licensing, and the perennial Irish question. Its energies were dissipated in party contests which were animated by sectarian bitterness and exploited by vested interests. The advanced wing of the Labour movement cared for none of these things. Although they were in a minority they were able to count upon the general feeling of disillusionment and the growing spirit of discontent which was in part due to the rise in the cost of living. The contention that Parliament was powerless to improve the conditions under which men and women did their daily work gained wider acceptance. Political democracy, it appeared, was a more or less empty form unless it could be combined with industrial democracy. From this criticism there emerged two ideas which are at the root of modern speculations about the future of industry. First, it was argued that representation, secured by means of elections on the most extended franchise within constituencies of a territorial nature, was not true representation. It cut across the real divisions of an industrial community and tended to reduce organized labour to impotence. Second, it was demanded that the producers should have a greater control over industry through bodies elected by themselves, thereby substituting a constitutionalism for the autocracy which capitalists had hitherto enjoyed. These ideas assumed a variety of forms in the complete systems put forward by advocates of ultimate solutions; but they are more significant as an expression of a point of view which influenced many who had no interest or faith in newfangled theories.

Those who maintain that political institutions are, either through their very nature or because they can easily be corrupted, useless as instruments of genuine industrial reform are thrown back on the existing industrial organizations. Here they are confronted by the difficulties inherent in the present structure of trade unionism. The movement has a long history in this country and retains many marks of the stages through which it has passed. There are, for instance, some 1120 separate unions; a fact which in itself explains the practical impossibility of common action.[1] The older unions are made up of skilled men who unite to further the interest of their craft. They were unwilling to merge their identity in a larger union with a broader basis. Effective common action, however, would seem to depend on the reduction of the number of unions and the adoption of some new principle of organization. This is the policy of the Industrial Unionists. They argue that the

[1] This number is often contrasted with the fifty trade unions in Germany; the figures are not strictly comparable, but the difference they suggest is substantially true. For historical reasons Germany has fewer and better organized unions.

fact of the concentration of industry on the capitalist side should be recognized, and a corresponding unification of the forces of labour effected. As against the craft union, which includes men who are engaged on some single process without regard to the industry it subserves, they advocate an industrial union, which would cover all who are employed in an industry without regard to the particular process, skilled or unskilled, they perform. Such a union would embrace, for example, all who are employed in railway transport, which may be regarded as a distinct industry. The railway companies would thus be faced by one great union which would be well suited to conduct successful strikes. For Industrial Unionism is essentially aggressive, and strikes are conceived as incidents in a general campaign.

The reduction of the number of trade unions by promoting federation or amalgamation of the existing unions is a natural consequence of the growth of larger aggregations of capital. The marshalling of forces on one side and the other raises the question of ultimate aim. Are the two parties to come to some agreement by which they are equally represented on an industrial council to which is entrusted a general supervision of the industry concerned? Or are they necessarily antagonistic? If there must be war, what are the fruits of victory? These are questions which may be discussed but cannot be answered. In attempting to characterize the opinions held by the advanced thinkers in the ranks of labour—and therefore the ideas which were becoming familiar to an ever-increasing number of working men—it must be admitted that a contest in which labour was ultimately successful was assumed as inevitable. The Industrial Unionists, it has been noticed, intend to have no compromise. But a more complete conception of ultimate purpose is found in the writings of Syndicalists and Guild Socialists. Syndicalism is French in origin, arising as a protest on the part of organized labour against the division and ineffectiveness of political Socialism. It has never won much support in England, though its doctrines are in many respects only precise formulations of ideas more loosely held in this country. The claim that the producers should have control of industry is made absolute; they are to have sole control through their industrial organizations not only of all production but also of the State itself. All bodies formed on the basis of local representation, such as Parliament and the municipal corporations, are to disappear; for the principle of representation of consumers is regarded as vicious. The industrial character of the community is therefore fully recognized and all its institutions are made to rest on it. There is no longer any distinction between political and industrial action because political has no meaning. Syndicalists propose to achieve their ends by means of strikes, culminating according to some of them in the General Strike, and by a great variety of forms of sabotage. They accept the Class War as a fact, and found their economic analysis on the right of the producer to the whole product. No novelty can be claimed for these views; what is new is the professed intention to dispense with the kind of representative institutions which were evolved in the nineteenth century in favour of bodies representing the workers employed in the various industries. This was carrying the anti-parliamentarianism of these years to its logical conclusion. Guild Socialism, however, attempts to secure complete self-government in industry for the producers without destroying the present representative bodies; it sets side by side the organizations of consumers, founded on residence in a common locality, and of producers, based on a common function. The ownership of the means of production is ascribed to the State as representative of the consumers, while the actual conduct of industry is entrusted to National Guilds of producers. These guilds are to enjoy immunity from any external interference with their affairs. They are to include all who are engaged in the industry, the members are to elect their managers, and they are to share the reward of their service to the community on principles determined by themselves. All the guilds are to be represented at a Guild Congress which is to be co-equal with Parliament, and ultimate power in case of dispute is to rest with a Joint Committee of Congress and Parliament. Guild Socialism, it is claimed, reconciles the interests of consumers and producers by giving equal weight to the political and the industrial point of view. It may be doubted, however, whether the dualism which it accentuates does not present greater difficulties than the Syndicalist refusal to recognize, or at least to tolerate, any clash of interest between consumer and producer.

While these opinions were making some headway among the rank and file of the Labour movement the very basis of direct Labour representation in Parliament was threatened by an important legal decision. The Labour Party, it will be remembered, is a political organization formed by the Socialist societies and certain trade unions.[1] A large proportion of its representatives in the House of Commons are trade union officials. Their candidature and maintenance as Members of Parliament involved expenses which were in part met out of

[1] The miners' representatives did not join the Labour Party until 1910, when they abandoned their Liberal-Labourism.

trade union funds. This arrangement was open to objections from two sections of the movement. Those who thought political action was of no value were naturally not enthusiastic about it; but a stronger protest came from the trade unionists who still clung to the old political parties. The matter was brought to an issue by W. V. Osborne, the secretary of a branch of the Amalgamated Society of Railway Servants, who opposed any contribution from the Society's funds or any levy of its members in support of the Labour Party, to which he did not personally owe allegiance. The House of Lords, as the final Court of Appeal, held that a trade union had no right to use any of its funds for political purposes. The "Osborne Judgment" (1909), indeed, was much more drastic in its effect than this. The judges, arguing that a trade union though not expressly incorporated by Statute must be regarded as in fact a corporation, declared that its powers are limited by the Act under the provisions of which it functioned. Consequently, they went back to the Trade Union Act of 1876 and decided that the words of definition amounted to a limitation. "The term *trade union*," runs the Act, "means any combination, whether temporary or permanent, for regulating the relations between workmen and masters, or between workmen and workmen, or between masters and masters, or for imposing restrictive conditions on the conduct of any trade or business, whether such combination would or would not, if the principal Act had not been passed, have been deemed an unlawful combination by reason of some one or more of its purposes being in restraint of trade." This confined a trade union to purely industrial activities; it ruled out the expenditure of money on education, municipal or national propaganda, and did not even recognize the administration of friendly benefits.[1] The judgment, whatever its merits as legal interpretation, paid no regard to the obvious facts of trade union history and practice. It did not merely protect members who had conscientious scruples against any part of their subscriptions going to the support of a political party to which they did not belong; it condemned political action on the part of a trade union even if its members were unanimously in favour of it. The Labour Party had to deal with the situation thus created. In this they were only moderately successful. According to the terms of the Trade Union Act (1913) a union may spend money on parliamentary representation, provided a majority of members taken by special ballot agrees and the fund is kept separate: the minority need not contribute, and the fact that it does not is not to prejudice its position within the union.

The opinions which were gaining wider acceptance in the years immediately preceding the War may be characterized as criticisms of the Collectivist ideal. When it was contending against the dominant Individualism Collectivism had the great advantage of being able to expose the inadequacies of that creed in the face of pressing social problems. But success revealed its own weaknesses. Collectivism had always insisted on the organic nature of Society, and therefore had tended to endow its instruments, whether the State or the Municipality, with extensive powers. The democratic nature of these institutions seemed to qualify them for the proper discharge of social functions. It was, indeed, the belief that the extensions of the franchise had

[1] The position was somewhat relieved by the Resolution of the House of Commons in favour of the Payment of Members (1911), which, it will be recalled, was one of the "points" of the Charter.

established popular sovereignty which reconciled the Individualists to the growth of State intervention. The conception of the State as something external gave place to the conception of it as the means by which the common will found expression, and consequently the antithesis between the individual and the State was blurred or denied to exist. Individualists had also to admit that their doctrine of freedom of contract was not applicable in a great number of important instances because the parties to the contract were not really free. The State had therefore to interfere to secure genuine equality in bargaining. Along these lines some kind of agreement between Individualists and Collectivists was possible. Each side, for instance, came to support Factory Acts, Truck Acts, and Workmen's Compensation Acts, and, though their theoretical reasons were different, the result was that Collectivism appeared to have gained a complete ascendancy. But correctives immediately began to operate. The desirability of State control was questioned. Collectivism, according to some, would lead to the rule of efficient bureaucrats whose energetic organization of the community would amount to a tyranny more complete, because more intelligent, than had ever been endured in the past. Others pointed out that Collectivism, working through bodies representative of the consumers, would be chiefly concerned with questions of distribution. The special interests of producers might be neglected; for nationalization of the means of production, which the Collectivists advocated as a solution of the industrial question, would not necessarily give those actually employed any greater degree of control than they had under private enterprise.

The case against the Collectivist solution is stated with much ingenuity by Hilaire Belloc in his *Servile*

State (1912). He admits that the Collectivist is working with the grain of Society, but contends that the attempt to provide security and sufficiency for all by State action would involve so much regimentation that in the end freedom would be destroyed. The drift towards the Servile State is clearly indicated, in his opinion, in the legislation which gives the proletarian *quâ* proletarian special protection, because it substitutes status for contract. As examples he adduces the Insurance Act and the proposals in favour of a minimum wage; these are attempts to palliate the insecurity of the proletarian. It is no part of his thesis to consider whether the control of industry by the producers would counteract the tendencies which he discovers in Collectivism. His own solution is the Distributive State which would restore to the majority the possession of property, of which they have been deprived by the development of capitalism. The objections to Collectivism which are involved in the theories of Syndicalists and Guild Socialists have already been noticed. They are not comparable with the argument maintained in the *Servile State,* except in one particular: there is strong suspicion of the activities of the State. The advocates of control of industry by the producers, however, demand organization and regulation; but they entrust such powers to a functional and not to a territorial representation of the people.

How Collectivism would have been modified by these criticisms, had not the country been involved in the War from 1914 to 1918, it is impossible to say. It had certainly not entered on its decline. The principle of the minimum wage, which it had consistently upheld in the face of the opposition of accepted economic teaching, was recognized in the Trade Boards Act (1909) and the Coal Mines (Minimum Wage) Act (1912). In the former instance, the Board of Trade was empowered to apply the Act to a specified trade, if it was satisfied that the rate of wages was exceptionally low as compared with that in other employments.[1] Trade Boards were set up in a number of trades, of which the most notable were chain-making and ready-made tailoring. These and other trades which were brought under the Act were examples of sweated industries with no organization on the part of the workers. The Coal Mines Act, however, applied to one of the most effectively organized industries in the country. It was demanded by the Miners' Federation of Great Britain and the demand was backed by a prolonged national strike. Parliament accepted the principle in this case with great reluctance as a way out of a difficult position. But such an extension of minimum wage legislation could not fail to have a profound effect on the public attitude towards the question. The course of legislation is a sufficient indication of the general acceptance of Collectivist ideas. For an example of its method of dealing with a great social question it would be well to study the Minority Report of the Royal Commission on the Poor Laws (1909). If this document be compared with the Poor Law Report of 1834 some very definite contrasts between Individualism and Collectivism emerge. Both display the logical completeness of inquirers who have a thorough grasp of the first principles of their theory. The Commissioners of 1834 have no conception of poverty

[1] This has been extended by the Trade Board Act (1918), which may be applied "if no adequate machinery exists for the effective regulation of wages throughout the trade." The Trade Board has taken its place in the scheme for the organization of industry recommended by the Whitley Committee. The establishment of Trade Boards is now in the hands of the Minister of Labour. See pp. 175–6.

as a social phenomenon, the causes of which are to be sought by a careful analysis of society.[1] They are mainly concerned with so restricting relief that it will only be given in the extreme instance. They endeavour to make it so unpleasant that a person will endure a great deal before applying for it. Obviously they supposed that in most cases personal effort would make such application unnecessary. The authors of the Minority Report, on the other hand, approach the question from the social point of view; poverty is for them a social disease rather than a demonstration of original sin. They refuse to accept the principle that a pauper taint attaches to those who receive relief. So, while the Commissioners of 1834 recommended the establishment of a special destitution authority, the Minority Commissioners of 1909 advocated the "break-up of the Poor Law," that is, the abolition of the Boards of Guardians and the distribution of the functions, which they discharge for paupers only, among the public authorities which perform similar duties for the non-pauper population. The charge of all children they ascribe to the local Education Authorities, of all aged to the local Pension Committees, of all sick to the local Health Authorities; thereby eliminating the present overlapping and removing a cross division based on the differentia of destitution. This proposal rests on the recognition of the development of local government in the nineteenth century: in 1834 such bodies did not exist and the

[1] This is fully recognized in the historical outline which prefaces the Majority Report (vol. i. p. 109). "It (the Report of 1834) does not lay down, or proceed on, any philosophical theory of the place of poverty in the social organism, of rights to life or to work, even of the duty of the State towards its less fortunate members, except in one particular that, where the State gives relief, it should make the situation of the able-bodied recipient less eligible than that of the independent labourer."

setting up of an *ad hoc* destitution authority might be justified. The Minority Report also deals very fully with unemployment, under which term what was known as able-bodied pauperism in 1834, and long after, has come to be included. This change is very significant. In 1834 able-bodied pauperism seemed largely a matter of individual fault, and consequently machinery was adopted which would induce the recipients of relief to seek work. The Minority Report regards unemployment as a function of industry which can only be dealt with by organized effort. They claim that it can be prevented by so arranging the work undertaken by public authorities that in times of depression the reserve of labour will be absorbed.

The first fourteen years of the twentieth century are destined to be regarded as an extension of the nineteenth century and a prelude to the Great European War. Historians will therefore find it peculiarly difficult to estimate their significance. Some may be tempted to stress the appeal to violence, which was a feature common to the Labour "unrest," the Suffrage movement, and the opposition to Home Rule, as a sign that some great upheaval was inevitable. Others may take seriously the view that the people were given up to frivolity, having lost their grasp of great issues and forfeited their right to control their own destiny. Under the stress of the war hard things have been said of pre-war society, but a fuller experience of post-war conditions will probably leave us with the feeling that the war which changed so much left a great deal unchanged. The war precipitated more problems than it created, and Reconstruction is an eternal social necessity.

SUPPLEMENTARY CHAPTER

1914–1918

IT is certainly premature to attempt to add anything of historical value on the social and industrial reactions of the period 1914–8. The events are so recent and conditions were so abnormal that it would be difficult enough to form a judgment if the facts were available; as they are very largely in the possession of the various Government Departments and, as far as the public knows, unsifted, it is only possible to offer a few generalizations and to suggest tentative conclusions.

The outbreak of war in August 1914 subjected the organization, social, industrial, and financial, to a strain which revealed its weakness and its strength. There was at the outset an almost complete dislocation, particularly in the financial sphere, and emergency measures had to be adopted to stimulate the operation of machinery which at ordinary times performs functions of which most of us are curiously ignorant. During the first three or four months there was a general sense of bewilderment; men caught at phrases which seemed to give them some assurance that the earth was not slipping from underneath their feet. To some the motto "Business as usual" seemed to indicate an attitude worthy of our traditions for coolness and common sense; to others, of a more sensitive temperament, some comfort was found in the persuasion that this was a "war to end war." All were agreed in congratulating one another on the new-found unity which the peril had produced. It is to the credit of the people that they were unable to face the facts. They were in themselves so appalling and in their working out so disastrous that the human mind could not appreciate their meaning or foresee their consequences. But prophecies were popular. It was so hard to believe that no one could know what was going to happen. It was even more difficult for some people to refrain from pretending that they knew. So prophecies about the possible duration of the war were seriously heeded, the general impression being that the interposition of some force, not clearly defined, would bring matters to a conclusion in a comparatively short time. This mood served to cover the transition from peace to war. In its various forms it must be regarded as a kind of protective illusion which was unconsciously adopted to save the mind from the full shock of the reality. The feverish desire to do something was another aspect of the same feeling.

In the spring of 1915 the implications of the war were generally accepted. The first impulsive reaction against the facts had spent itself, and the inexorable demands of the war began to fashion opinion to its requirements. The plea that "there is a war on" seemed to justify the extension of State control to a point hitherto not dreamed of and to require deep inroads upon the rights of individuals. Steps were taken to organize all the resources of the country for the prosecution of the war. Great armies were built up by voluntary recruiting, ultimately supplemented by conscription. To supply the armies with the equipment necessary for the conduct of modern warfare industry had to be revolutionized. Under the stimulus of the demand wielded by the Government by means of its prodigious war expenditure the whole community had its energies directed to one purpose. By its very nature that purpose was a temporary one. It became increasingly clear to reflecting persons that within a comparatively short time the demand would cease. On that day the machine would be running with such momentum that it seemed possible that the " outbreak of peace " would subject the country to a strain not unlike, and, possibly as severe as, that of 1914. Consequently, there emerged the problem of Reconstruction, which attracted considerable attention during the later phases of the war. There was a general agreement that a return to the *status quo ante* was neither possible nor desirable. But it must be confessed that there was no very clear understanding of what was to be substituted for the old system which it was held had proved itself incapable of providing the conditions of a decent life for large sections of the community. Reconstruction involves definite plans and intelligent and continuous effort. It is not a beneficent process to which persons who differ widely in their ultimate aims can agree in giving moral support. The belief that the old system was doomed to extinction and the quite laudable desire to have " a land fit for heroes to live in," merely raised fundamental social and industrial questions. Their solution was not to be found by evading contentious issues.

This rough summary of the development of opinion during the war suggests that a treatment of the period should consider the problems presented by the beginning, the middle, and the end.

In August, 1914, financial problems seemed the most urgent and difficult. Although Norman Angell's *Great Illusion* (1910) had done something to familiarize the ordinary reader with the wonders of the international ramifications of finance, the immediate collapse of the credit system greatly puzzled him. To some it appeared a decisive event; to others a demonstration of the essential unsoundness of the existing financial organization. This was to misread the significance of the crisis. The credit system was based on the assumption that the normal conditions of peace and competition would continue; and it had adapted itself to the requirements of those conditions. When they were destroyed the system necessarily collapsed. It did not follow, however, that a system could not be devised which would suit the new conditions. There are ways and means of financing a war so long as the belligerents can secure the requisite commodities to supply the bare wants of their armies and civilian population. Money can be too easily created for the lack of it to frustrate the will to conquer. War finance, from the peace point of view, may be extravagant and unsound, but there is no justification for the hope that these considerations will exercise any profound influence. Ever since it has been possible to finance wars by means of loans and the manipulation of the currency the same kind of blunders have been made. This suggests that forces are at work which overrule the recognized principles of sound finance. War in this sphere, as in others, is a pathological condition. No remedy can be discovered by an elaborate diagnosis of the normal function of the healthy subject.

It is impossible to explain in a brief summary the financial phenomena of August, 1914. The rise in the Bank rate from 3 to 10 per cent within a few days, the adoption of the Moratorium, the closing of the Stock Exchange, and the issue of "emergency currency" were the main features of the crisis. The joint-stock banks were pressed by their customers at a moment when the assets which they held against their obligations could not be realized. The machinery of the foreign exchanges broke down, and consequently acceptors of bills of exchange could not meet them on maturity. It was necessary for the Government to come to the assistance of the banks and the accepting houses. The old remedy was to allow the Bank of England to issue notes in excess of the limit prescribed in the Bank Charter Act of 1844. This was not considered adequate, and immediate steps were taken to issue Treasury notes for one pound and ten shillings. The new currency relieved the situation. It was now possible to make payments and postpone a general settlement until the situation became clearer. The introduction of paper money as an emergency measure may have been inevitable. The danger was that it would be found so convenient that it would be indefinitely retained. No limit was set on the issue of notes by the Government, though they were nominally convertible into gold at the Bank of England. The financial crisis therefore left as its chief legacy paper money which was virtually inconvertible.[1]

The temporary breakdown in finance was contemporaneous with a general dislocation in industry. This also is to be explained by the fact that industry was organized on the assumption that peace

[1] A lucid explanation of what occurred in the first few months will be found in *War and Lombard Street*, by Hartley Withers (1915). For the consequences of the abandonment of the gold standard see J. Shield Nicholson's *Inflation* (1919).

was the normal condition. The collapse of the mechanism of international exchange immediately affected foreign trade. Within the country the sudden cessation of demand, particularly in certain luxury trades which employed women, precipitated the problem of unemployment, which at first seemed to be going to present a serious and even permanent difficulty during the war. The extent to which the conduct of the war would create a demand for labour was not realized until the following year. In the first place, therefore, there was a considerable amount of unemployment, which was partly relieved by Distress Committees and partly by voluntary recruitment. Some indication of the coming effect of war on industry was supplied by the fact that recruiting could easily outpace the rate at which the army could be equipped. Experience was to prove that in industry war conditions meant that shortage, whether of skilled labour or of necessary materials, is the dominating consideration.

The immediate result of the declaration of war was an industrial truce. For some months before August, 1914, there had been ominous signs of "unrest" among the workers. It seemed to the optimists that these particular difficulties were now eliminated. And until the beginning of 1915 their hopes appeared to be justified. Then prices, which had suffered a temporary rise during the first month of the war, began to display a steady upward tendency. Particular attention was drawn to wheat and coal, and the suggestion was freely made that dealers were taking advantage of the situation to exact high profits. The Government resisted the suggestion of the Labour Party that prices should be controlled, for it held that a case had not been made out for departing from the principles of supply and demand. This attitude revived industrial unrest, which now took the form of demanding a rise in wages to meet the increased cost of living. An agreement between the railwaymen and the companies, entered into in February, 1915, virtually decided the method by which the advances would be made. Men earning less than 30s. a week were given a "war bonus" of 3s., those earning more than 30s. were to have 2s. This bonus was not calculated on any basis of the rise in the cost of living. It was also sharply distinguished from a permanent increase in the rate of wages. The war bonus principle, which was thus initiated, became a widespread movement. It came to cover, though never equally, nearly the whole field of industry, the well-organized workers reaping the advantage of their superior bargaining power.

It soon became obvious, however, that industry would not adjust itself to the requirements of the war without the more active intervention of the Government. In February, 1915, a Committee on Production in Engineering and Shipbuilding Establishments had been appointed to consider how the productivity of such establishments might be increased. The Committee made a number of recommendations which foreshadowed the great changes industry was to experience in the next three years. Relaxation of trade union rules and machinery to prevent stoppage of work deserve special mention. The former was negotiated at the Treasury Conference in March, when members of the Government met representatives of the chief trade unions concerned. "Any departure during the war," ran the agreement, "from the practice ruling in our workshops, shipyards, and other industries prior to the war shall only be for the period of the war." As for the latter, the Government gave the Committee of Production itself power to arbitrate on disputes which the parties agreed to refer to it. This arrangement was made more definite by the Treasury Agreement in March, the parties to it agreeing to refer differences to arbitration. Although the Committee on Production was not the only body to which disputes could be taken, considerable recourse was made to it. The findings of the Committee came to cover a wide range of subjects affecting practically every industry in the country.

The arrangements arrived at by the Treasury Conference were incorporated and defined in the Munitions of War Bill, which conferred extensive powers on the newly constituted Ministry of Munitions. The area of compulsory arbitration was made as wide as possible ; provision was introduced for the exercise of control over specified establishments ; the abrogation of trade union conditions was to some extent balanced by the limitation of profits. The Ministry of Munitions was the creation of the First Coalition Ministry : it was the first emergency Ministry called for by the circumstances of the war. To the end it remained not only the most highly organized but also the most potent in its influence on the development of industry. It was set up to exploit to the full the possibilities of production. There was a " market " for its products which could not be overstocked, and the cost was relatively immaterial. Consequently, its operations effected what may almost be called an industrial revolution.

The main lines of this revolution may be briefly illustrated from the mere necessities of the occasion. The men on whose shoulders the burden of industry normally falls were in increasing numbers withdrawn from productive employment to meet the demands of the fighting forces. At the same time there was a call for an enormously great output of material. The practical problem thus presented was met (*a*) by introducing new classes and grades of labour, women forming an important element; (*b*) by adopting various devices to increase the output per head, such as the suspension of trade union rules, the use of semi-automatic and automatic machines, experiments in new methods of management, payment by results, good time-keeping bonuses, etc.; (*c*) by the standardization of products. The pressure of these changes was peculiarly apparent in the individual workshop. There the implications of "dilution" of labour were obvious. The blurring of the lines of distinction between the skilled, the semi-skilled, and the unskilled was bound to arouse some misgivings. The employment of so many women on work which they had hitherto not attempted, and the fatigue induced by monotonous labour and long hours raised questions of health and welfare. These facts—and the surrender of the strike weapon by the trade unions—brought the shop stewards into prominence. In many instances Works Committees, on different models and with various functions, were established.[1] A new impetus was thus lent to the demand for the control of industry by the workpeople actually engaged in its conduct. Speculations which were abroad before the war now seemed likely to be realized.

The extent to which the ideas which were thrown up by the industrial unrest of the three or four years preceding the war were winning their way was revealed by the reports of the Commissions on

[1] A valuable report on the establishment and functions of Works Committees was published by the Ministry of Labour in 1918. See *Industrial Reports*, No. 2 (H.M. Stationery Office, price 6d.).

Industrial Unrest in 1917. The Commissioners for Wales and Monmouthshire found that the workers were developing a strong class consciousness. "The influence of the advanced men," they stated, "is growing very rapidly, and there is ground for belief that under their leadership attempts of a drastic character will be made by the working classes as a whole to secure direct control by themselves of their particular industries."[1] The Commissioners recommended that an effort to remove the immediate grievance of the high price and imperfect distribution of food should be made by granting Government subsidies. For the better working of industry they urged that some form of internal government should be set up on the lines of the suggestions of the Whitley Report.

This was a reference to the Interim Report of the sub-committee on the relations between employers and employed which had been appointed by the Reconstruction Committee. The sub-committee was of opinion that the circumstances of the time offered a great opportunity for securing a permanent improvement in the relations between employers and employed, while they feared that failure to utilize the opportunity might involve the nation in grave industrial difficulties at the end of the war. The recommendations contained in the Interim Report—more generally known as the Whitley Report from the name of its chairman—were accepted by the War Cabinet, and the newly constituted Ministry of Labour was instructed to take steps to make them as public as possible and to co-

[1] The country was divided into seven areas for inquiry and report. The Report of the Welsh Commissioners is particularly useful, because they did not confine themselves to temporary causes of unrest, but endeavoured to put the whole problem in its proper setting. See *Commission of Inquiry into Industrial Unrest: Wales and Monmouthshire*, Cd. 8668.

operate with the proper organizations in establishing the machinery they contemplated. So we pass from the industrial policy which was directed to the effective prosecution of the war to the adumbration of an official reconstruction policy. The first Whitley Report (usually referred to as *the* Whitley Report) recommended the setting up of bodies representative of the organizations of the employers and the employed in all suitable industries. These Joint Standing Industrial Councils, on which the two sides were to have equal representation, were to consider matters affecting the progress and well-being of their respective industries and to assist the Government by stating their needs and opinions to its Departments. An Industrial Council was therefore to be an authoritative body with a broader basis than any existing organization in the industrial world and with functions which could be extended to cover the whole conduct of the industry. It was expected to devolve some of its duties on Districts Committees, which were also to be representative of organizations of employers and employed; and Works Committees representative of the management and the workers were to be established in individual works. The joint organization would thus be preserved from the works right up to the national Industrial Council.

These recommendations were a recognition of principles which had long been discussed. They proposed to introduce into the management of industry a kind of constitutional government in the place of the autocracy, tempered by trade union action and legal enactments, which had hitherto been predominant. To some extent they might be claimed to be a reply to the request by the workers for the control of industry. But, it must be confessed, they were not received with any great enthusiasm. It should be noticed that an Industrial Council can only be set up when both sides are organized. There must be employers' associations and trade unions before the initial steps can be taken, because an Industrial Council is composed of representatives of these bodies. This limits the field very considerably; in practice it was further limited by the determination of such strongly organized workers as the miners and the railwaymen to remain outside. For the rest, there were employers who did not welcome any suggestion of trade union participation in the discussion of the policy of the industry. They were suspicious of the effect of the operation of Works Committees, pointing out that the younger men of extreme views might dominate them and aim at embarrassing rather than assisting the firm. Many trade unionists, on the other hand, felt that the joint machinery would in practice weaken the unions as fighting units by so closely associating their representatives at every stage with the employers. Others denounced the proposals as an attempt to perpetuate the wage system, which they wished to abolish; in fact, as a compromise which would strengthen the position of capitalism. Joint control was characterized as a sham, for, it was contended, labour could not secure any genuine control of industrial affairs through the agency of a composite body.

In spite of these and other difficulties, a number of Industrial Councils (51 at the present time) have been established in industries employing over 4,000,000 workers. It must be remembered, however, that whatever success attended the efforts to form such councils the problem of unorganized labour would be left untouched. The sub-committee addressed itself to this in their second report. They attempted to distinguish three types of industry, namely, those in which organization was reasonably complete, those in which it was less complete, and those in which organization was weak or even non-existent. It was discovered that it was difficult to define the qualification for the second category. The proposed classes were therefore reduced to two. The first class included the industries to which the machinery of the Industrial Council is applicable; the second, those to which it is not. For the latter, an extension of the Trade Board Act of 1909 seemed to offer the best solution. There are, of course, important differences between an Industrial Council and a Trade Board. An Industrial Council is voluntary in its character, and can only be brought into existence with the agreement of the employers' associations and the trade unions concerned. It enjoys extensive powers in deciding on its own functions and methods. A Trade Board, however, is a statutory body, established by the Minister of Labour in accordance with Regulations made by him in pursuance of the Trade Board Acts (1909 and 1918). While an Industrial Council is composed entirely of representatives of employers' associations and of trade unions, every Trade Board includes a number of "appointed members" unconnected with the trade and nominated by the Minister of Labour. The primary function of a Trade Board is to determine a minimum rate of wages, which, when it is confirmed by the Minister of Labour, becomes part of the law of the land and can be enforced by legal action.

These schemes for organizing industry seemed calculated to supply something which the Government discovered to be lacking when it had to improvise an industrial policy in the course of the war. Common sense, it could be argued, required that the lessons of the war should be learnt, and that we should not enter upon the period of reconstruction in an unorganized condition. There would be questions relating to the absorption of demobilized men in industry, and the disposal of the surplus stores the Government would have in hand at the end of the war. The promise that trade union conditions should be restored would present difficulties, because its literal redemption would mean the abandonment of many practices which had spread their roots deep in the new methods of production.[1] The whole bonus system would come up for review. In the face of these and other problems of the end of the war, organization seemed essential if widespread industrial trouble was to be avoided. The formation of Industrial Councils and Trade Boards demanded more time than was likely to be forthcoming. It was therefore arranged that the Minister of Reconstruction should assemble Interim Industrial Reconstruction Committees to advise him on the immediate questions which arose. These Committees were in due course to give place to the more permanent bodies already described.

The achievements of organization during the war have already been referred to; they were notable, but they were obtained under special conditions. As a guide to the treatment of after-war problems they are likely to prove somewhat misleading. Two examples may be noticed. The Control Board in the Woollen and Worsted Industries succeeded in organizing industries which were very imperfectly organized. It undertook its work because the Government had to clothe the army, and the normal method of doing so by competitive tender

[1] On this problem consult the *Restoration of Trade Union Conditions* (1917), by Sidney Webb.

was no longer practicable. At first the War Office Contracts Department had experimented by requisitioning the output of certain factories at a price which was calculated to cover cost of production and reasonable profits. But the enormous increase in the Government demand soon revealed a shortage in the raw material. To assure itself of a sufficient supply the Government decided to buy up the whole home and Australian yield in 1916. It had now to undertake the rationing of the industry with wool, that is, to decide what proportion was to go for civilian use and whether the export trade was to be specially considered. To deal with these delicate questions the Control Board was instituted. It consisted of thirty-three members—eleven Government officials, eleven spinners and manufacturers, and eleven trade unionists. "Not the least important of its functions was the means that it has afforded for employers, workpeople, and officials to meet together with executive responsibility for the settlement of wide trade and national issues raised in connexion with the Wool Textile Industry. In spite of the difficulties of short supplies of raw material, the Board secured, by means of rationing of wool to spinners and yarn to manufacturers, what has never been assured in the industry before —even employment throughout the trade." [1] This experiment, difficult as it was in many respects, was simplified by the fact that, when the Government requirements were met, less than 20 per cent of the output of the trade was left for civilian uses. The advantage of having one great customer, which was also the owner of the whole supply of raw material, must also be kept in mind. The Cotton Control Board offers some suggestive contrasts with these condi-

[1] *The War Cabinet Report for the Year 1918*, pp. 210–1 (Cd. 325).

tions. The industry was already much more highly organized. In fact, it was the elaborate organization and the extreme localization of cotton manufacture that made it necessary for the Government to intervene. Here it was not primarily a matter of supplying Government needs, but of preventing a serious crisis in one of the most important industries of the country. The shortage of raw cotton threatened to drive up prices to an unprecedented height. The Board of Trade therefore closed the Liverpool Cotton Exchange and arranged that prices of American cotton should be fixed from day to day at a rate which would allow for transport, insurance, and a reasonable profit for the broker. The Cotton Control Board consisted of sixteen members, of whom six represented employers' associations, four trade unions, two the Board of Trade, and four commercial organizations. The Board met the shortage of American cotton by restricting the spinners of it to the use of a proportion of their spindles. There was a good supply of Egyptian cotton, and the users of it were allowed to employ all their spindles provided they paid a levy on the percentage in excess of those running in mills where American cotton was spun. A similar method was adopted in dealing with the manufacturers, a levy being imposed on those who used more than 60 per cent of their looms. The levies provided a fund to maintain the workpeople who were unemployed on account of the restrictions. Unemployment pay was administered by the trade unions, whether those who received it were members of the unions or not. This scheme might be applicable to other than a war emergency. It is based on the recognition of the fact that the industry is an essential unity. Full responsibility for the operatives is accepted, and the trade unions are recognized as the proper authorities for administering unemployment benefit.

Experiments such as these established a strong presumption in favour of organization. It was discovered that where employers and employed had their representative bodies the Government had a means by which they could at once come into touch with the industry. The ideal that every employer should have his association and every workman his trade union seemed worth striving to attain. It was at the back of the official schemes for Reconstruction. Experience alone will show how far one can argue from the examples provided by the special circumstances of the war period. The problems of different industries have to be closely considered. Suitable machinery might conceivably be devised in every instance and organizers may be justified of their offspring; but we live in a world of men and women who will always be apt to mar the finest of their schemes and strive, however blindly, to achieve something nearer to the heart's desire.

APPENDICES

APPENDIX A.—CONSPECTUS OF

THIS table is a general analysis of the argument followed in the text. is fully discussed in Dicey's

Character of Government.	Dominant Attitude of Government.	Regulation of Industrial Conditions.
—1832.—HOUSE OF COMMONS unreformed and unrepresentative.	**Old Toryism** (Paternal) { (*a*) Benevolent. (*b*) Repressive.	Health and Morals of Apprentices' Act (1802). Factory Act (1819).
REFORM ACT (1832). — Enfranchisement of the Middle Class. REFORM ACT (1867). — Enfranchisement of the artisans in the boroughs.	**Laissez-Faire.** { (*a*) Pure Individualism. (*b*) Modified by Humanitarianism.	First important Factory Act (1833). — Children and young persons in textile factories. Factory Act (1844). —Women protected. 1856. —First Act which gave any protection to adult males—fencing of machinery.
REFORM ACT (1885). — Enfranchisement of the agricultural labourers in the counties.	**Collectivism.**	Great extension of Factory Legislation to cover hours, meal-times, ventilation, escape from fire, etc. etc.

The whole question of the relation between legislation and opinion
Law and Opinion in England.

Association of Wage-earners.	Relief of Poor.	Trade Policy.	Municipal Government.
Combination Laws of 1799 and 1800.	"Speenham-land" system of relief in aid of wages (1795–1834).	Protective (complex tariff). Corn Law of 1815.	Unreformed Boroughs.
Repeal of Combination Laws in 1824 and 1825.	Poor Law Amendment Act (1834).	Peel's Budgets of 1842 and 1845. — Simplification of tariff. Repeal of the Corn Laws (1846). Gladstone's Budgets of 1853 and 1860. — Completion of Free Trade.	Municipal Corporation Act (1835). — Representative.
Trade Union Act (1871). Conspiracy and Protection of Property Act (1875).	Amelioration of the treatment of different classes— 1. Aged. 2. Children. 3. Unemployed (mostly administrative reforms).	*Reciprocity.* *Fair Trade.* *Tariff Reform.* (unsuccessful reactions against Free Trade.)	Great extension of municipal enterprise: water, light, drainage, transport, parks, art galleries, museums, etc. etc.

APPENDIX B

A LIST OF BOOKS

THE following list does not pretend to be a Bibliography of the subject. I have gone on the principle of only admitting the titles of books to which I am conscious I owe some particular obligation.

There are three books which deal with general aspects of the subject: (1) Slater's *Making of Modern England* (Constable & Co.); (2) Perris' *Industrial History of Modern England* (Kegan Paul, Trench, Trubner, & Co. Ltd.); and (3) Cressy's *Outline of Industrial History* (Macmillan & Co. Ltd.). The last section of Meredith's *Outlines of the Economic History of England* (Sir Isaac Pitman & Sons Ltd.) and the last three lectures of Ashley's *Economic Organisation of England* (Longmans, Green, & Co.) also contain a general treatment. Most of the remaining books are concerned with special aspects of the subject, which are sufficiently indicated by their titles. The excerpts in Bland, Brown, and Tawney's *Economic History: Select Documents* (G. Bell & Sons) do not come beyond the middle of the nineteenth century.

ASHLEY, SIR WILLIAM J.—*The Economic Organisation of England.* (1914.)

BARKER, ERNEST.—*Political Thought in England, from Herbert Spencer to the Present Day.* (Home University Library.)

BEER, M.—*A History of British Socialism,* Vol. I. (1919.) (An expansion of the Author's *Geschichte des Sozial-*

ismus in England which was published in 1912. Vol. I. covers the period down to 1834.)

BLAND, BROWN, AND TAWNEY.—*Economic History: Select Documents.* (1914.)

CARLYLE, E. I.—*William Cobbett.* (1904.)

COLE, G. D. H.—*The World of Labour.* (1913.)

Labour in War-Time. (1915.)

Labour in the Commonwealth. (1919.)

CRESSY, EDWARD.—*An Outline of Industrial History.* (1915.)

CROTCH, W. WALTER.—*Charles Dickens: Social Reformer.* (1913.)

CUNNINGHAM, W.—*The Growth of English Industry and Commerce.* Part I. "Modern Times"; Part II. "Laissez Faire." (1912.)

CURTLER, W. H. R.—*A Short History of English Agriculture.* (1909.)

DICEY, A. V.—*Law and Public Opinion in England.* (1905.)

DOBBS, A. E.—*Education and Social Movements, 1700–1850.* (1919.)

DOLLÉANS, EDOUARD.—*Le Chartisme, 1830–1848.* (1912.)

FIRTH, C. H.—*Then and Now, or a Comparison between the War with Napoleon and the Present War.* (Creighton Lecture for 1917.)

FUCHS, CARL JOHANNES.—*The Trade Policy of Great Britain and her Colonies since 1860.* (English translation, 1905.)

GRETTON, R. H.—*A Modern History of the English People.* Vol. I. 1880–1898; Vol. II. 1899–1910. (1913.)

HAMMOND, J. L. AND BARBARA.—*The Village Labourer, 1760–1832.* (1912.)

The Town Labourer, 1760–1832. (1917.)

HOBHOUSE, L. T.—*Democracy and Reaction.* (1904.)

HOBSON, JOHN A.—*The Evolution of Modern Capitalism.* (1906 Edition.)

John Ruskin: Social Reformer. (Third Edition, 1904.)

HOVELL, MARK.—*The Chartist Movement.* (1918.)
HUTCHINS, B. L., AND HARRISON, A.—*A History of Factory Legislation.* (1911.)
KIRKUP, THOMAS.—*A History of Socialism.* (1906.)
LAYTON, W. T.—*An Introduction to the Study of Prices, with special reference to the History of the Nineteenth Century.* (1912.)
LLOYD, C. M.—*Trade Unionism.* (1915.)
MACDONALD, J. RAMSAY.—*The Socialist Movement.* (Home University Library.)
MACGREGOR, D. H.—*The Evolution of Industry.* (Home University Library.)
MANTOUX, PAUL.—*La Révolution Industrielle au XVIIIe Siècle : Essai sur les commencements de la grande industrie moderne en Angleterre.* (1906.)
MARVIN, F. S.—*The Century of Hope : A Sketch of Western Progress from 1815 to the Great War.* (1919.)
MENGER, ANTON.—*The Right to the Whole Produce of Labour.* (1899.)
MEREDITH, H. O.—*Outlines of the Economic History of England : A Study in Social Development.* (1912.)
MORLEY, LORD.—*Life of Richard Cobden.* (1881.)
NICHOLSON, J. S.—*The History of the English Corn Laws.* (1904.)
Inflation. (1919.)
PEASE, EDWARD R.—*The History of the Fabian Society.* (1916.)
PERRIS, G. H.—*The Industrial History of Modern England.* (1914.)
PODMORE, FRANK.—*Robert Owen : A Biography.* 2 vols. (1906.)
PORTER, G. R.—*The Progress of the Nation.* (Porter's work was first published in 1836 and 1838 in separate parts ; a second edition appeared in 1846, and a third in 1851. A completely new edition revised and brought up to date was prepared by F. W. Hirst and published in 1912.)
RUSSELL, BERTRAND.—*Roads to Freedom : Socialism, Anarchism, and Syndicalism.* (1918.)

SLATER, GILBERT.—*The Making of Modern England.* (1914.)
SMART, WILLIAM.—*Economic Annals of the Nineteenth Century.* Vol. I. 1801–1820. (1910.) Vol. II. 1821–1830. (1917.)
TOYNBEE, ARNOLD.—*Lectures on the Industrial Revolution.* (New Edition, 1908.)
WALLAS, GRAHAM.—*The Life of Francis Place, 1771–1854.* (Revised Edition, November 1918.)
WEBB, SIDNEY AND BEATRICE.—*The History of Trade Unionism.* (New Edition, 1911.)
WEBB, SIDNEY.—*Towards Social Democracy? A Study of Social Evolution during the Past Three-quarters of a Century.* (1916.) (A reprint, with notes, of the Author's contribution to the "Cambridge Modern History," Vol. XII.)
WITHERS, HARTLEY.—*The War and Lombard Street.* (1915.)

INDEX

For Product Safety Concerns and Information please contact our EU representative GPSR@taylorandfrancis.com
Taylor & Francis Verlag GmbH, Kaufingerstraße 24, 80331 München, Germany

www.ingramcontent.com/pod-product-compliance
Ingram Content Group UK Ltd.
Pitfield, Milton Keynes, MK11 3LW, UK
UKHW022156190926
475702UK00003B/59
* 9 7 8 1 0 3 2 1 8 2 7 8 0 *